*Dedicated to action-oriented people everywhere
who are making wise choices to save our planet
for the benefit of the generations who will inherit it.
Be of good courage and know you are not alone!*

Other Titles in the Sustainable Practices Series

Sustainable Practices: Your Handbook for Effective Action
Bite-sized Changes, Big Impact: Your Sustainable Food Journey
Creating Wonderful Waste: Your Guide to Sustainable Composting
Money That Matters: Your Guide to Sustainable Finances

To learn more, please visit us at
www.SustainablePractice.Life

Your Earth Share

Seven Pathways to Sustainable Living

2025 Edition

Fred Horch

Peggy Siegle, Editor

SUSTAINABLE PRACTICE

Copyright © 2025 by Sustainable Practice

All rights reserved

First Edition, 2025 revision 1.0.16

Published by Sustainable Practice
Brunswick, Maine, USA

Publisher Contact:

Sustainable Practice
P.O. Box 255
Brunswick, Maine 04011
www.SustainablePractice.Life

ISBN: 979-8-9928169-1-4

Available through:

Leanpub • Amazon • Ingram Spark

Available formats:

Paperback • Portable Document Format • Kindle

Categories:

1. Environmental protection–Citizen participation
2. Sustainable living–Handbooks, manuals, etc.
3. Green technology–Popular works
4. Home economics–Environmental aspects

This book is part of the Sustainable Practices series, providing evidence-based guidance for meaningful environmental action. Visit our companion web app at www.suspra.com for interactive tools, calculators, and additional resources.

Table of Contents

Introduction: Your Environmental Budget 1
   The Numbers Are Sobering 2
   We're Pushing Past Planetary Boundaries 2
   Your Power to Create Change 3
   Seven Pathways to Sustainability 4
   Twenty High-Impact Practices 4
   How to Use This Book 5
   Share This Book with Friends and Family 5

Pathway #1: Community 7
   Why Start with Community 7
   The Power and Responsibility of Knowledge 8
   Put on Your Own Oxygen Mask First 8
   A High-Impact Community Practice 9
   Toward a Sustainable Community 11
   Your Sustainable Community Dashboard 13
   Creating Waves 14

Pathway #2: Food 15
   Your Food Choices Shape Earth's Future 15
   Strategies for Sustainable Food 16
   High-Impact Food Practices 16
   Your Sustainable Food Dashboard 18
   Toward Sustainable Food Practices 19
   Common Concerns and Solutions 21
   Your Food Choices Change Our World 22

Pathway #3: Water 23
   Your Water Share in a Finite World 23
   Strategies for Sustainable Water Use 24
   High-Impact Water Practices 24
   Your Sustainable Water Dashboard 25
   Toward Sustainable Water Practices 26
   Common Concerns and Solutions 29
   Water Flows Through Everything 29

Pathway #4: Movement 30
   The Faster You Live, the Bigger Your Impact 30

    Strategies for Sustainable Movement 31
    High-Impact Movement Practices 31
    Your Sustainable Movement Dashboard 32
    Toward Sustainable Movement Practices 33
    Common Concerns and Solutions 35
    Your Movement Creates Your World 35

Pathway #5: Energy 37
    Your Energy Share of Earth's Balance 37
    Strategies for Sustainable Energy Use 38
    High-Impact Energy Practices 39
    Your Sustainable Energy Dashboard 42
    Toward Sustainable Energy Practices 43
    Common Concerns and Solutions 45
    Your Energy Transformation 45

Pathway #6: Goods 47
    Your Material Share of Earth's Abundance 47
    Strategies for Sustainable Material Flows 48
    High-Impact Goods Practices 49
    Your Sustainable Goods Dashboard 50
    Toward Sustainable Goods Practices 51
    Common Concerns and Solutions 53
    Today's Choices Create Tomorrow's World 54

Pathway #7: Habitat 55
    Your Share of Earth's Habitat 55
    Strategies for Sustainable Habitat 56
    A High-Impact Habitat Practice 56
    Your Sustainable Habitat Dashboard 57
    Toward Sustainable Habitat Practices 58
    Common Concerns and Solutions 61
    Your Habitat Makes the World Whole 61

Measuring and Planning Next Steps 63
    Your Sustainability Dashboard 63
    Measuring Where You Are 65
    How to Take Your Next Steps 67
    Financial Planning 68
    Making It Stick 71
    Family and Household Engagement 71
    Technology Tools 73
    From Measurement to Meaning 73

Your Personal Implementation Roadmap	74
The Compound Effect	75

Your Earth Share Wisely Used 76
Your Numbers Tell the Story	76
A Truth About Sustainability	76
Your Impact Is Already Multiplying	77
The World We're Creating	77

Appendix A: Your Earth Share 78
Planetary Math	78
What Your Earth Share Must Provide	79
The Power of Your Choices	88

Appendix B: Planetary Boundaries 89
How boundaries connect to your practices	90

Appendix C: Seven Pathways 91
Community Pathway	91
Food Pathway	92
Water Pathway	94
Movement Pathway	94
Energy Pathway	96
Goods Pathway	97
Habitat Pathway	99

Appendix D: Suggested Resources 102
Artificial Intelligence	102
Data	102
Environmental Frameworks and Projects	102

Preface

Welcome to *Your Earth Share*. You might have picked up this book because you're ready to take your next step toward sustainability. Or perhaps you're curious about what practical environmental action really looks like. Either way, you've found the right resource. Thanks for reading!

The seven pathways and twenty practices in this book work anywhere—apartments to houses, cities to suburbs. Many impactful changes—eating less meat, washing clothes in cold water instead of hot water, walking more—are easy to try, cost nothing, and save money.

In this edition, we share what we've tested and know works for homeowners in the United States. But we're also planning future editions:

- **An international edition** for diverse climates and cultures
- **A renter's edition** for those who can't renovate or build
- **An essentials edition** emphasizing free and money-saving practices for people on tight financial budgets
- **Regional editions** adapted to specific locations

If something doesn't fit your situation, consider the general principle behind it. Can't install solar panels? Support community solar. No yard? Find a composting drop-off. While this edition's examples focus on U.S. households with spending flexibility and control over their living spaces, the principles are universal.

Thank you for caring about our planet's future. Whether you implement every practice or try just one, you're contributing to positive change. Your Earth share is yours to manage wisely, in whatever way makes sense for your life right now.

—Fred Horch and Peggy Siegle
  Brunswick, Maine
  August 2025

P.S. Find something that needs adapting for your situation? Tell us at EarthShare@SustainablePractice.Life.

Introduction: Your Environmental Budget

When I'm tempted to buy something, I have a pretty good idea whether I can afford it. I know grabbing a coffee to go every day means less money for vacation, or that getting potatoes on sale frees up a few dollars for a splurge on organic chocolates. Every month, I can see exactly how my spending and savings add up. You probably have a similar grasp of your financial budget.

But what about your environmental budget? By virtue of our planet's size and population, you and I and everyone else have an environmental budget that's even more fundamental than our financial one. If we consume more per person than our environment can provide, we're not just jeopardizing our credit scores; we're risking the quality of life for everyone on Earth.

This book helps you understand your environmental budget and the impact of your choices, so you can translate your values into effective action to protect our planet. You'll learn how to spend and save environmental resources wisely and how to know whether you are living within your environmental means.

I give lots of talks and demonstrations. Afterwards, audience members will often come up to explain apologetically why they aren't doing more to save our planet. I sometimes feel like I'm doing environmental guilt therapy. I get it: I'm not doing everything I possibly could, either. No one is. And no one has to!

No one has to do *everything* if everyone does *something* to help save our planet. Reading this book is a fantastic first step. Lending it to friends is a superb second step. Getting together to discuss it is a terrific third step. Then, with your new knowledge and growing community, you can take more steps that make sense for you.

The point of this book isn't to tell you what you should or shouldn't be doing. Instead, it's to empower you to act according to your core values. What personal practices make you proud?

The Numbers Are Sobering

Our planet's size of 51 billion hectares and population of 8.2 billion people determine your environmental budget—an *Earth share* roughly the size of a soccer field of habitable land (depending on how you define habitable) plus an expanse of ocean and uninhabitable land. This represents your portion of Earth: how much is available to meet *your* needs without infringing on the inalienable right of other people to meet *their* needs. (For the detailed math behind this calculation, see Appendix A.)

Unless hampered by unsustainable practices, your Earth share is constantly replenishing the resources you require. You have a sustainable plan if your Earth share can supply your food, the materials you use, the energy that powers your life, the water you use for drinking, bathing, and washing, and the space required to process all your waste—year after year. This aspect of sustainability isn't about money or political power. It's about respecting the carrying capacity of spaceship Earth.

Earth's human population will probably top out around ten billion people and then decline after 2080. Because of population growth (more people sharing the same planet), your Earth share is smaller than your parents' was, and just a little bigger than your children's will be. Your challenge is to be environmentally wiser than your parents were and teach your children to be wiser than you are.

We're Pushing Past Planetary Boundaries

Scientists have identified nine *'planetary boundaries'*—critical Earth systems that sustain human life. Although not everyone agrees about the data and interpretation, researchers have gathered mounting evidence that we've pushed six of these systems beyond safe limits, while three are in the safe zone but still require vigilance to remain out of danger. (For complete definitions and how your practices connect to each boundary, see Appendix B.)

Of the nine processes, climate change gets most of the attention, but we've also polluted and consumed our way past safe limits for biosphere integrity, biogeochemical flows, land-system change, freshwater change, and novel synthetic substances. We're only at a safe level for substances that deplete ozone in our stratosphere, aerosols that cloud our air, and pollution that acidifies our oceans. This book explains what you can do in your home to help all nine critical processes return to and remain at safe levels.

Your Power to Create Change

Planetary problems like climate change may seem too massive for you to influence. But no matter how skeptical you are about individual action compared to systemic pressures, I invite you to learn your options and consider what personal effect you would like to have on nature and society.

Solar power became the major source of new electricity capacity in the United States because early adopters proved it worked, and then investment and policy changes followed. Organic food became mainstream because environmentally conscious consumers ate it, and then more farmers grew it. Dozens of models of electric vehicles are available now because a few drivers leased and bought early versions, proving that battery-powered vehicles could find a market. Generating electricity from sunlight, growing food in ways that build healthy soil, and getting around without burning fuel are moving the needle in a positive direction on planetary boundaries.

Your choices can tip the scales toward a more hospitable natural environment for everyone. To take just one example, keeping ocean acidification in the safe zone will require using solar, wind, or water power instead of burning fossil fuel. You decide when you will make the transition to clean energy in your own home.

If you feel the call to go beyond being a savvy consumer to becoming an environmental champion or policy advocate, practicing sustainability yourself makes it more likely your leadership will inspire followers. When you demonstrate *how* to be more environmentally sustainable, you won't be dismissed as just a naïve activist. Your ideas will have the weight and benefit of real-world, science-based, first-person experience behind them.

Seven Pathways to Sustainability

Improving your practices (how you meet your needs) can be steps on a journey to a world that works better for everyone—with clean air and water, a stable climate, abundant biodiversity, and thriving communities. Sustainability indicators for your community, food, water, movement, energy, goods, and habitat show how far along you are on your journey.

The seven pathways interconnect beautifully. Improving along any one of them makes progress easier in others. Eat more plants, and you'll save water and energy. Walk or cycle more, and you create opportunities for community connection.

Twenty High-Impact Practices

Of the myriad sustainable steps you *could* take along each pathway in your home, twenty practices matter most.

1. Grow a community that practices environmental sustainability.
2. Compost biodegradable solid waste.
3. Walk, cycle, or take public transit for local errands.
4. Eat more plants and little or no domesticated red meat.
5. Plant a food garden or buy from local organic farmers.
6. Drink more water and fewer bottled beverages.
7. Clean with safe products in minimal packaging.
8. Recycle metal, clean cardboard, and glass; avoid plastic.
9. Seal and insulate attics, basements, and exterior walls.
10. Use LED lighting with motion sensors and daylight dimming.
11. Landscape with native plants using organic methods.
12. Wash clothes in cold water in an efficient machine.
13. Heat domestic water using electric heat pumps.
14. Dry clothes in a condensing dryer, on racks, or on lines.
15. Keep food cold in energy-efficient refrigerators and freezers.
16. Cook with induction ranges and convection ovens.
17. Drive an electric car when you can't walk, bike, or go by bus.
18. Use electric heat pumps for space heating and cooling.
19. Generate solar electricity on-site or subscribe to a solar farm.
20. Flush water-efficient toilets.

Throughout the following chapters, you'll find each of these twenty high-impact practices clearly explained and identified with this step-up icon.

How to Use This Book

This book serves as a focused, practical guide for turning your environmental values into effective action. Each pathway chapter is self-contained, so start wherever you like. To build knowledge and relationships that supply ongoing support, begin with community. To save money with practices that *conserve resources* (using less by simply giving up comfort or convenience) or invest money to earn a financial return with practices that *increase efficiency* (using fewer resources thanks to better technology or techniques), check out the food, water, or energy chapters.

Learning how to spend or save our finite yet replenishing planetary resources transforms your relationship with the world. Go from feeling overwhelmed to having clear priorities and actionable steps. Move beyond wondering whether your choices matter to tracking your measurable progress.

Two things make this book stand out from other books about sustainable living. First, you'll get a chance to see how climate change is just one of nine serious environmental challenges you can do something about. Your carbon footprint is important, but it's just one of many impacts to measure and manage for a sustainable future. Second, this book is tightly focused on practical actions under your control. Personal and political action aren't mutually exclusive; in fact, we believe they work well together. But our focus is on the personal. We leave it to other capable authors to share their wisdom about the realm of politics.

Share This Book with Friends and Family

Giving people the wisdom and courage to act is reason enough to share this book. But another reason is to recruit companions on your journey to sustainability. It's more fun and safer to be traveling as a group, all heading in the same direction, than shouldering the load alone, struggling against the crowd.

Read this book. Think about it. Share it with your spouse, best friend, children, or parents. Discuss it with your family and social circle. The more people in your closest community who understand how to become more environmentally sustainable, the more likely you'll all reach life-sustaining goals together.

Pathway #1: Community

Starting a Sustainable Wave

On July 30, 2025, water molecules in the Pacific Ocean started acting strangely. Each one moved just a seemingly insignificant distance—perhaps a few centimeters. But because every molecule tugged and pushed on its neighbors, together they were remarkable. An 8.8 magnitude earthquake off Russia's remote Kamchatka Peninsula put these molecules in motion. Within hours, the waves it generated had traveled thousands of miles, triggering tsunami warnings from Japan to Hawaii to Chile.

Like individual water particles moving just a little, but tightly connected to others, your individual environmental actions that seem small can have a massive impact as interactions ripple through your community. Your personal choices—composting garbage that can rot, switching to LED lighting, walking instead of driving—are tiny compared to challenges like global warming. But in the right place at the right time, your actions contribute to waves of transformation that reshape entire societies.

Without individual movement, waves don't happen at all. Every great environmental success story—from the recovery of our ozone layer to the mainstream adoption of solar power—began with an individual like you who decided to act.

Why Start with Community

One molecule moving by itself isn't a wave, but neither are many molecules moving randomly. Uncoordinated motion creates heat; it doesn't transmit power. It's only when water molecules move in the same direction at the same frequency that they create powerful waves.

The same principle applies to environmental action. Random steps—you buy a new electric vehicle while your neighbor pours money into keeping a gas-guzzler on the road—have no collective power. But when you show your community how to protect our planet, you help actions become coordinated and powerful.

This is why growing a community that practices environmental sustainability is our foundational practice. Your environmental impact isn't just about your personal choices. It's about making wise practices resonate for positive change in your community.

The Power and Responsibility of Knowledge

Before you dive into action, know that misguided measures, no matter how well-intentioned, make environmental problems worse. Take California's plastic bag ban, implemented in 2014 with the noble goal of reducing plastic waste. The policy seemed straightforward: ban thin plastic shopping bags and charge for thicker plastic bags to encourage people to use less plastic. But when the thin bags disappeared, people bought additional thicker plastic bags. The result: the weight of plastic waste in California landfills per person actually *increased* by 44%.

This doesn't mean environmental laws are pointless—quite the opposite! California learned from this experience and passed a new, improved plastic bag ban in 2024 that closed loopholes. The lesson here is that success depends on understanding the systems we're affecting and measuring the results of our actions.

Put on Your Own Oxygen Mask First

Flight attendants tell us to secure our own oxygen mask before helping others. The same principle applies to sustainability. Once you have reviewed and improved your own practices, then you can wisely advocate for others to change their practices.

This isn't about being perfect—nobody's sustainability practices are flawless. It's about authenticity and insight. When you've installed solar power, you know what to ask contractors and what obstacles others might face. When you've composted for a season, you can share what works and what doesn't. When you've tried living car-free for a year, you fully appreciate both the benefits and the challenges. Firsthand experience makes you a better advocate, role model, and community builder.

A High-Impact Community Practice

Grow a Community That Practices Sustainability

This foundational practice operates through three interconnected strategies: understanding sustainability, demonstrating best practices, and nurturing positive relationships.

Build Your Knowledge Foundation

Ground your actions on solid, science-based knowledge of how human activities affect Earth's life-support systems. Learn which practices actually make a positive difference. Grasp fundamental concepts well enough to make wise decisions and explain them to others. When someone asks why you're composting, going solar, or taking another environmental action, be able to give a clear, factual answer that inspires them to follow your lead.

Start with the fundamentals:

- **Nine planetary boundaries**: The critical Earth processes that sustain human life
- **Your environmental budget**: A soccer field of habitable land plus some ocean and inhospitable land to meet your needs, the same as everyone else
- **Twenty high-impact practices**: The practical steps you can take at home to deliver the biggest positive impact

Keep reading this book to comprehend these fundamentals so you can pass a science-based knowledge quiz with ease!

Lead by Example

When you demonstrate sustainable best practices consistently and well, people see that you're not just pretending to care about environmental protection—you're living it. They also witness that you're not making huge sacrifices for the sake of ideological purity but finding better ways to meet *your* needs that allow them to meet *their* needs, too.

Your demonstration laboratory includes:

- **Your home**: Energy efficiency, clean power, water conservation, non-toxic materials
- **Your movement**: Walking, cycling, planning trips
- **Your consumption**: Less waste, more reuse, quality over quantity, composting, and recycling materials you've used
- **Your landscape**: Native plants, organic methods, habitat protection, restoration, and enhancement

Start where you are, with what you have, taking action that aligns with your values, interests, and resources.

Nurture Your Network

Develop connections that support mutual learning and action. Some friends will be ahead of you on certain pathways to sustainability—learn from them. Others will be just starting their sustainability journey—share what you've discovered. Most people can appreciate some aspects of sustainability but feel threatened by other aspects—seek common ground.

Relationship-building happens through:

- **Sharing information**: Forwarding articles, discussing documentaries, recommending books
- **Volunteering together**: Going on environmental cleanups, doing community garden work, and making home repairs
- **Celebrating progress**: Giving awards, acknowledging milestones, hosting parties
- **Problem-solving collaboratively**: Organizing buying groups, sharing tools, and troubleshooting challenges

Make sustainability social and positive rather than preachy and judgmental. Provide fun, friendship, and mutual aid.

Toward a Sustainable Community

Community begins at home. Do something to help yourself or someone else take a step toward sustainability. Here are a few ideas: for hundreds more, see our comprehensive reference work, *Sustainable Practices: Your Handbook for Effective Action*.

This Week: Quick-Start Practices

Start a personal sustainability journal. Begin documenting your own sustainability journey in a paper or digital journal. Note what you're learning, what challenges you're encountering, and why you're on the journey.

Your sustainability journal serves as both a thinking aid and a conversation starter. When people ask about your sustainability efforts, you'll have specific experiences and goals to discuss.

Calculate your sustainability score. Assess your own knowledge, practices, and social interactions by using our sustainability score calculator at www.suspra.com. This isn't a test you can pass or fail—it's a chance to find out what you really know, what you really do, and how you interact with other people in your community. (See more on the scoring framework in Appendix C.)

Don't worry if you score lower than you'd like. Everyone starts somewhere. Acknowledging gaps in your understanding and practices is the first step toward filling them. Use your results to prioritize efforts and track improvement over time.

This Month: Building Better Habits

Set your sustainability goals. Are you as sustainable as you want to be? What next step would make the biggest impact?

- Community
    - Knowledge quiz: Novice to expert
    - Practice survey: 0% to 100% best practices
    - Volunteer log: Social zero to community hero
- Food
    - Clean plate: Garbage galore to zero waste

- Bottled beverages: 0% to 100% tap water
- Eco-friendly menu: 0% to 100% eco-friendly
- Plant-based meals: Meat-heavy to completely vegan
- Sustainable source: 0% to 100% regeneratively grown
- Water
  - Flow rate: Water wasteful to water-wise
  - Pollution rate: Problem property to model home
- Movement
  - Average speed: Jet setter to local explorer
  - Travel modes: Fuel-burning to human-powered
- Energy
  - Average power: Energy wasteful to energy efficient
  - Electricity share: 0% to 100% electrified
  - Solar share: 0% to 100% solar powered
- Goods
  - Consumption rate: Shopaholic to thrifty mender
  - Circular economy: 0% to 100% compostable or recyclable
  - Healthy materials: 0% to 100% non-hazardous
  - Waste management: 0% to 100% composted or recycled
- Habitat
  - Occupancy rate: Low to high
  - Building standards: None to many green certifications
  - Conservation area: None to vast tracts
  - Native species: 0% to 100% naturally occurring
  - Nutrient load: Large excess to zero excess
  - Pest control: 100% synthetic chemicals to 100% organic

Use our online tools to set goals and create a personalized action plan that makes the best use of your time and resources.

Share environmental knowledge. Find one fact-based article about sustainability and share it with someone in your family or friend network who cares about our environment. Choose something genuinely relevant to their interests—energy costs for a budget-conscious friend, air quality for someone with asthma, or local farms for a foodie.

Include a brief personal note about why the article made you think of your family member or friend but keep it short and sweet. The goal is to spark curiosity and conversation, not to convince or convert. Seek opportunities to get an honest reaction and build goodwill, prioritizing your relationship above any difference of opinion or lack of interest in a topic.

Join a local environmental volunteer project. Search for environmental volunteer opportunities in your area—river cleanups, tree plantings, community garden work, or energy audit programs. Participate in one project this month to protect our environment, meet like-minded people, and gain hands-on experience with sustainable practices.

Your Sustainable Community Dashboard

Here's where results get real: your community dashboard indicators show how well you're growing a community that practices environmental sustainability. Use our online tools to check where you are now, then decide whether you want to improve.

> ***Measuring Your Progress:** At www.suspra.com you'll find optional online tools for evaluating your sustainability and personalizing guidance to your specific situation, all for free. To use a tool, you can type the link into a web browser or point your smart phone's camera at the box of dots for the QR code.*

How well do you understand sustainability?

Can you score 80% on a Sustainable Practice knowledge quiz? www.suspra.com/score/knowledge	

Your Earth Share

How well are you demonstrating sustainable practices?	
Can you do all high-impact practices well? www.suspra.com/score/practices	

How well are you nurturing relationships?	
Can you volunteer 100 hours per year in your community? Can you exchange knowledge with someone every day? www.suspra.com/score/interactions	

Creating Waves

Growing a community that practices sustainability is a rewarding process of learning, demonstrating, and connecting. Your individual actions, however small they might seem, are part of something much larger. The difference between doing nothing and doing something is actually huge. Zero multiplied by billions is still zero. But a tiny positive action, when multiplied by billions of people, becomes an irresistible force.

Start where you are, with the people you know, using the knowledge and resources you currently have. Begin with practices that align with your values and interests. Share what you learn. Connect with others who share your commitment to a more sustainable future. Launch a powerful wave. Who knows what distant shores it will reach!

Pathway #2: Food

Nourishing People and Planet

If you can choose what to eat, you hold a voting franchise unlike any other. Every time you take a bite, you're determining which farming practices win more territory dedicated to feeding you.

Farmers produce what they can sell. Food companies supply what moves off shelves. Eating local eggs for breakfast? You're steering the use of our planet's productive land toward small-scale farming. Buying a beef burger for lunch? You're pumping hundreds of gallons of precious water from your Earth share to livestock systems that push multiple planetary processes into the danger zone.

If you have food choices—a privilege not everyone enjoys—you have an influential voice in how agricultural land will be allocated. This chapter shows you how to use your power wisely.

Your Food Choices Shape Earth's Future

Consider your Earth share, the share of our planet that gives everyone an equal and inalienable right to life, liberty, and the pursuit of happiness. If you eat plant-based meals, all the crops you need can grow in your Earth share—with plenty of room left over. But if you eat meat-based meals, four times more of your Earth share must be devoted to agriculture—and most of that land will be used to feed animals, not you.

How we humans choose to produce our food currently breaches six of the nine planetary boundaries that determine whether Earth will stay in the safe zone for our long-term survival. Our collective dietary preferences are pushing us beyond safe limits for climate change, biosphere integrity, land-system change, freshwater change, biogeochemical flows, and novel synthetic substances. The encouraging news: we know how to feed more than ten billion people within safe planetary boundaries if we choose to eat plant-based diets.

Strategies for Sustainable Food

Along the food pathway, four interconnected strategies wisely allocate your Earth share:

Steward food resources and reduce food waste by understanding expiration dates, buying only what you can eat, storing food properly, and eating leftovers rather than throwing them out. When you prevent food waste, you maximize the value of the land, water, and energy that went into growing, harvesting, packaging, and shipping food for you to eat.

Choose eco-friendly ingredients that have lower environmental impacts than close substitutes. For example, *Katsuwonus pelamis* (skipjack tuna) populations are healthy worldwide, whereas most *Thunnus thynnus* (bluefin tuna) populations are overfished.

Eat plant-based meals more often than animal-based ones. It's more efficient to use land to grow plants that people can eat, rather than to provide pasture or feed for beef and dairy cows.

Cultivate healthy harvests by growing your own food or buying from regenerative farmers who enhance soil health, protect biodiversity, and build resilience in food systems.

 ## High-Impact Food Practices

Eat More Plants and Less Domesticated Red Meat

The single most powerful dietary change you can make is reducing your consumption of beef, lamb, and other "red meat" (i.e., meat from animals that chew their cuds). An easy way to start is by reducing the amount of meat you add to pasta, rice, and tortilla meals. Plant-based proteins like peas, beans, lentils, tofu, and nuts deliver complete nutrition while requiring dramatically fewer resources from your Earth share. Mediterranean and Asian cuisines offer thousands of years of culinary wisdom for creating satisfying plant-based meals.

If you choose to eat animals, smaller ones like chicken and fish are more sustainable than larger ones like cows and sheep.

Grow or Buy Food from Healthy Soil

Growing your own food—even herbs on a windowsill—gives you deeper insight into how healthy soil creates nutritious food and how farming practices can heal or harm ecosystems. Basil, parsley, cilantro, and mint grow easily in a sunny spot indoors and transform ordinary meals into delicious occasions. In a small outdoor space, container gardens on sunny patios and balconies can produce surprising amounts of food.

If growing food isn't practical for your situation, shop at farmers markets where you can ask growers directly about their practices. Buy food from farms that build soil health, protect water quality, and provide habitat for wildlife. If you can, join a Community Supported Agriculture (CSA) program to receive seasonal produce from a local regenerative farm.

Drink More Water and Fewer Bottled Beverages

Drinking more tap water, in communities with safe water supplies, is probably the easiest way to improve your environmental impact immediately while saving money every day. You avoid all the environmental costs of growing corn, barley, grapes, coffee, and other sweeteners, flavorings, and colorings found in sweetened, alcoholic, or caffeinated beverages. You save the cost of bottling, brewing, and distributing beverages. And you eliminate the packaging waste of beverage containers.

Beyond infancy, if you are healthy, you can meet all your hydration needs by eating a balanced diet and drinking water. A sustainable way to enjoy coffee, tea, juice, soda, and alcoholic beverages is to savor them as luxuries on special occasions. Drinking plain water as your regular habit reduces the pressure on your Earth share to keep up with your thirst.

Invest in quality reusable bottles so you can fill from a faucet and carry water with you. Municipal water systems in developed countries meet strict safety standards, but a simple filter can remove chlorine and make your water taste better. This setup costs pennies on the dollar compared to buying bottled beverages and prevents enormous amounts of plastic waste.

Your Sustainable Food Dashboard

Use our online tools to measure how well you can allocate your Earth share to produce the food and drink you enjoy.

> ***Measuring Your Progress:*** *At www.suspra.com you'll find optional online tools for evaluating your sustainability and personalizing guidance to your specific situation, all for free. To use a tool, you can type the link into a web browser or point your smart phone's camera at the box of dots for the QR code.*

How much food do you waste?	
Can you eat 95% of the food you purchase? www.suspra.com/score/foodwaste	

What do you drink?	
Can 80% of your drinks be tap water? www.suspra.com/score/beverages	

Seven Pathways to Sustainable Living

Are you choosing eco-friendly ingredients? *Are you eating plant-based meals?* *Are you supporting regenerative agricultural practices?*	
Can every meal ingredient be eco-friendly? *Can 80% of your meals be plant-based?* *Can 50% of your ingredients be local?* *Can 50% of your ingredients be organic?* www.suspra.com/score/meals	

Are you growing any of your own food?	
Can you grow one item to eat? *Can you garden without synthetic chemicals?* www.suspra.com/score/garden	

Toward Sustainable Food Practices

After you've assessed your current practices, you'll know how much food you waste, what you typically eat, and how your food is produced. Then, if you want to make changes, you can prioritize how to achieve the most significant positive impact. Here are some ideas for action. For many more ideas, see *Sustainable Practices: Your Handbook for Effective Action*.

This Week: Quick-Start Actions

Replace One Meat Meal with Plants. Choose a meal to be plant-based. Monday breakfast might become oatmeal with nuts and fruit instead of bacon and eggs. Wednesday dinner could feature bean and vegetable chili instead of beef stew. Friday could be vegan tofu paprikash over pasta instead of a cheese pizza.

Your Earth Share

Switch to Filtered Tap Water. Install a simple water filter on your kitchen faucet or use a filtered pitcher. Buy one high-quality reusable water bottle for each family member. If your family can kick the soda, beer, or coffee habit, you'll save hundreds of dollars annually while eliminating dozens of pounds of packaging.

Buy Organic. If you shop for food in a grocery store in the United States, look for the USDA Organic certified label on products.

This Month: Building Better Habits

Create a Weekly Meal Plan. Plan your meals before grocery shopping. Include breakfast, lunch, dinner, and snacks. Prevent overbuying to reduce food waste and ensure you have eco-friendly ingredients for healthy plant-based meals.

Master Food Storage Techniques. Learn to store produce properly so it lasts longer. Keep potatoes and onions in cool, dark places (but not together). Store tomatoes on the counter, not in the refrigerator. Wash and thoroughly dry leafy greens, then store in containers with paper towels to absorb moisture. See if you can thereby double the edible life of your fruits and vegetables by avoiding haphazard storage techniques.

Find Local Food Sources. Visit a farmers market and talk with growers about their practices to protect the environment. Join a Community Supported Agriculture (CSA) program to receive seasonal produce directly from a local farm that practices regenerative agriculture.

Build Your Plant-Based Recipe Collection. Start collecting plant-based recipes your family enjoys. Include quick weeknight meals, weekend projects that make great leftovers, and crowd-pleasers for entertaining. Focus on ingredients you can buy locally and seasonally. Prevent the "what's for dinner?" decision fatigue that leads to unsustainable choices.

This Year: Transformative Changes

Establish a Home Food Garden. Grow some of your own food. Start with herbs and salad greens—they're easy to grow and expensive to buy. Add tomatoes, peppers, and other favorites as your skills develop.

Achieve 80% Plant-Based Meals. Shift your eating patterns so that 80% of your meals feature plants and mushrooms as the stars, with meat, dairy, and eggs playing supporting roles. If you're already fully vegetarian or vegan, you've already surpassed this milestone!

Lead Community Food Programs. Organize a community garden or food waste reduction challenge. Host potluck dinners featuring local, seasonal, plant-based ingredients. Start a buying club for organic produce or partner with local farms for group purchases. Your leadership helps others allocate their Earth shares more wisely while building community resilience.

Common Concerns and Solutions

"Plant-based meals take too much time to prepare." Build a collection of quick plant-based recipes. Batch-cook grains, beans, and roasted vegetables on weekends for use during busy weekdays. Keep canned beans, frozen vegetables, whole grains, nuts, and good olive oil on hand to create countless satisfying meals with minimal prep time.

"My family won't eat vegetables." Serve more fruit, nuts, rice, quinoa, mushrooms, and pasta that taste better than vegetables to many people. Add finely chopped vegetables to pasta sauces, soups, and stir-fries. Roast vegetables with olive oil and salt to bring out their natural sweetness—many people who dislike steamed broccoli enjoy it roasted crispy. Invite your family to search for interesting plant-based meals and encourage them to help you prepare them.

"Organic food costs too much." Prevent food waste to save money, then use the savings to buy organic food. Buy "seconds" (produce with cosmetic blemishes) at farmers markets. Grow your own herbs or lettuce from seed without using synthetic chemicals.

"I don't have space to garden." Grow herbs and microgreens on windowsills. Participate in community gardens.

"I don't know how to cook without meat." Search online for videos, blogs, and recipes from people just like you who made the switch to plant-based meals. Everyone learns either by watching someone else or just trying things on their own and seeing what happens!

Your Food Choices Change Our World

When you prevent food waste, you honor the land, water, and human effort that went into growing that food. When you drink tap water instead of a sugary, alcoholic, or caffeinated beverage, you eliminate all the impacts of producing sweeteners, flavorings, and colorings, and making beverage containers, filling them, shipping them, and disposing of them. When you choose eco-friendly ingredients instead of eco-harmful ingredients, you protect biosphere integrity and ensure Earth's continued bounty. When you eat plants, you free up 75% of the agricultural land that would be necessary for you to dine on animal flesh. When you support regenerative farmers, you help sequester carbon in soil.

Eat healthy and nutritious food you enjoy, while aligning your diet with your values and circumstances. Your individual impact might seem small, but you're influencing a global market that determines how much food can be made available and affordable for everyone.

Pathway #3: Water

Flowing Through Life

As you read these words, water from the last rainfall in your neighborhood has already rushed through storm drains and reached the nearest river or stream on a journey that could take it hundreds of miles downstream in a few days, to the ocean within months, and back to the clouds where it might fall as snow on a distant mountain next year. The water flowing through your home is part of an endless cycle that connects your daily choices to watersheds, aquifers, and ecosystems worldwide.

Water stewardship isn't just about the money you're spending on your water bill or private well. It's about being a wise guardian of water on its travels, using only what you need, keeping it clean, and returning it safely to the cycle that sustains everyone.

Your Water Share in a Finite World

Here's a harsh reality: water is unevenly distributed across our planet, and we're rapidly depleting the easy sources. Of Earth's vast water supply, only a tiny fraction is freshwater accessible through rivers, lakes, and shallow groundwater. (For detailed water cycle calculations and sustainable water budgets, see Appendix A.)

Pollution compounds scarcity. Water's nature as a "universal solvent"—its ability to dissolve more substances than any other liquid—makes it uniquely vulnerable to contamination. As the old saying goes, add a drop of sewage to a gallon of clean water and you have a gallon of sewage. Whether it's agricultural fertilizers, industrial chemicals, or household cleaners, contamination spreads far beyond its source through interconnected systems.

Your daily choices matter because water connects everything. Your dietary choices determine whether a trickle or a flood of water is required to grow the plant and animal products you eat. Your cleaning products flow into the same water cycle that supplies drinking water. Your water conservation at home allows you to live on renewable rainwater without demanding fossil groundwater.

Strategies for Sustainable Water Use

Along the water pathway, three interconnected strategies help you become a wise guardian of this precious resource. Don't fall for the trope that protecting the environment requires sacrificing comfort or convenience. *Resource efficiency* (adopting clever ways to consume less while maintaining your quality of life) is just as valid an approach as *resource conservation* (giving up convenience for the greater good). Most people find success combining both approaches—upgrading technology when possible and striving to moderate consumption.

Optimize water efficiency by investing in better techniques and technology that let you use less water without reducing your standard of living. For example, a WaterSense showerhead maintains excellent pressure while using 30% less water—you get the same satisfying shower experience with better environmental performance.

Conserve water by making conscious choices to reduce your consumption, accepting some discomfort or inconvenience for environmental benefit. Taking shorter or fewer showers saves water by simply foregoing consumption rather than increasing efficiency.

Protect water quality by choosing carefully what goes down your drains. Non-toxic cleaning products, proper disposal of hazardous materials, and landscape practices that prevent runoff ensure you return clean water to the cycle. This strategy can involve both efficiency (using concentrated cleaners that work better) and conservation (cleaning less frequently).

 High-Impact Water Practices

Clean with Safe Products in Minimal Packaging

Cleaning your home is a chance to decide about which substances will enter your local water cycle. When you spray a counter, mop a floor, or wash clothes, those chemicals go down your drain—either to your septic system and then your local soil and groundwater, or to a wastewater treatment plant and then your regional river, lake, or ocean.

Choose plant-based, biodegradable cleaning products that break down safely in water systems. Avoid synthetic antibacterial chemicals like triclosan that persist in the environment and contribute to antibiotic resistance. Skip products with synthetic fragrances and dyes that serve no cleaning purpose but add chemical complexity to manufacturing and to wastewater treatment.

Buy concentrated products to maximize environmental benefits. Add tap water to concentrate instead of using many bottles of ready-to-use product, reducing both plastic waste and transportation impacts.

Flush Water-Efficient Toilets

In most North American homes, toilets account for more than 25% of indoor water use. Older toilets use up to seven gallons per flush, while WaterSense-certified toilets use 1.28 gallons or less while maintaining excellent performance. Over a toilet's 20-year lifespan, an efficient model can save a family of four more than 38,000 gallons of water compared to an older toilet.

If replacing toilets isn't immediately feasible, simple retrofit toilet bank bags or adjustable flappers can save a gallon or more per flush. But be careful with some DIY solutions like bricks or bottles in the tank—these can interfere with proper flushing and actually waste water if you need to flush twice. If you do anything to reduce the amount of water your toilet tank holds, just check that you're actually saving water as a result.

For the truly committed, waterless composting toilets eliminate flush water entirely while creating valuable compost for landscaping. Though beyond the scope of consideration for most families, they are the pinnacle of water conservation in sanitation.

Your Sustainable Water Dashboard

Use our online tools to monitor how wisely you're using and protecting this precious resource.

Your Earth Share

Measuring Your Progress: At www.suspra.com *you'll find optional online tools for evaluating your sustainability and personalizing guidance to your specific situation, all for free. To use a tool, you can type the link into a web browser or point your smart phone's camera at the box of dots for the QR code.*

How much water do you use daily?	
Can you stay under 40 gallons per person per day? www.suspra.com/score/flow	 Flow

Are you protecting water quality?	
Are all your cleaning products biodegradable? *Do you properly dispose of hazardous materials?* www.suspra.com/score/pollution	 Pollution

Toward Sustainable Water Practices

Once you understand your current water use patterns, you can prioritize changes that deliver the biggest impact. Here are a few ideas; for many more, check out *Sustainable Practices: Your Handbook for Effective Action.*

This Week: Quick-Start Actions

Hunt for Hidden Leaks. Check your water meter before bedtime, then again first thing in the morning without using any water. If the meter has moved, you have a leak. A single leaky toilet can waste more water than most people use for all other purposes combined. Put food coloring in a toilet tank to see if your flapper leaks and check faucets and visible pipes for obvious drips.

Install WaterSense Fixtures. Replace old showerheads and faucet aerators with WaterSense-certified models. These simple screw-on devices cost a few dollars each but can reduce water flow by half while maintaining excellent pressure. Installation takes minutes and requires no special tools.

Switch to Eco-Friendly Cleaning Products. Replace harsh chemicals with plant-based, biodegradable alternatives. Look for products certified by Green Seal, EcoLogo, or similar third-party standards. Concentrated formulas reduce packaging and eliminate filler ingredients.

Take Shorter Showers. A standard showerhead uses 2.5 gallons per minute, so cutting just two minutes from your shower saves 5 gallons. Set a timer or play a favorite song to keep track. Navy showers—water on to get wet, off while soaping up, on again to rinse—can reduce shower water use by 50% or more.

This Month: Building Better Habits

Upgrade to Efficient Appliances. When replacing washing machines or dishwashers, choose ENERGY STAR models that use up to 40% less water than standard models. Front-loading washing machines typically use less water than top-loaders and clean more effectively. Modern dishwashers use less water than hand washing.

Master Smart Water Habits. Wait for full loads before running dishwashers and washing machines. Skip pre-rinsing dishes—modern dishwashers handle food residue effectively. Fix leaky faucets promptly—a single drip per second wastes 3,000 gallons annually. Turn off the water while brushing teeth, shaving, or washing hands— this doesn't save that much water, but it helps you keep your water consumption in mind every day.

Install Rainwater Collection. Set up rain barrels to capture water from downspouts for landscape irrigation. A single inch of rain on a 1,000-square-foot roof yields 600 gallons of water. Use harvested rainwater for gardens, car washing, and other non-potable uses. This reduces demand on municipal water systems while preventing runoff that can be polluting.

Create Water-Smart Landscaping. Choose native plants that thrive on natural rainfall in your region. Group plants with similar water needs together and mulch heavily to retain soil moisture. Install drip irrigation or soaker hoses for efficient watering when needed. Eliminate or reduce lawn areas that require regular irrigation.

This Year: Transformative Changes

Install Greywater Systems. Capture water from bathroom sinks, showers, and washing machines for landscape irrigation. Simple laundry-to-landscape systems can be installed for a few hundred dollars and immediately reduce both water consumption for landscaping and wastewater production. More complex systems can handle multiple sources but require professional installation and local permits.

Achieve 100 Liters (26.4 Gallons) Per Day. Through efficient fixtures, smart habits, and water-conscious landscaping, work toward the global sustainability target of 100 liters (26.4 gallons) per person per day for all household uses. This challenging but achievable goal puts you well within planetary boundaries for freshwater use while demonstrating what's possible with current technology and mindful consumption.

Lead Community Water Conservation. Organize neighborhood leak detection workshops, rain barrel building events, or native plant exchanges. Partner with local water utilities to promote rebate programs for efficient fixtures. Advocate for green infrastructure projects like rain gardens and permeable paving that help communities manage stormwater naturally.

Common Concerns and Solutions

"Water is cheap, so why worry about conservation?" Even where water is abundant and inexpensive, conservation reduces strain on infrastructure, protects ecosystem flows, and builds resilience for drought years. Saving water also reduces energy consumption for water treatment and distribution, cutting both costs and emissions from energy systems.

"Efficient fixtures don't provide enough pressure." Modern WaterSense-certified products undergo rigorous performance testing to ensure they deliver satisfying pressure and coverage while using less water. Look for products with high user ratings and consider trying different models if your first choice doesn't meet expectations.

"Greywater systems seem too complicated." Start with simple laundry-to-landscape systems that require no electrical components or storage tanks. As you gain experience and see benefits, you can expand to more sophisticated systems. Many areas have trained installers who can design systems appropriate for your local climate and regulations.

"My homeowner association won't allow rain barrels or native plants." Document the environmental and economic benefits of water conservation practices, then work with your association to update restrictive policies. Partner with neighbors who share your interest in water stewardship to present unified proposals.

Water Flows Through Everything

By becoming a wise steward of water in your own home, you're contributing to the health of watersheds and ecosystems far beyond your property boundaries. The water flowing through your home today has fallen as rain on mountains, nourished forests, sustained wildlife, and may have quenched the thirst of countless creatures before reaching your tap. Honor that journey by using it wisely and returning it to the cycle as clean as possible.

Pathway #4: Movement

Evolving Transport

An American travels 40 miles per day on average—a feat that would have astonished our forebears. We've built a world where daily commutes traverse distances that once defined epic journeys. But this high-speed lifestyle isn't always making us happier or wealthier. In many ways, it's making us more stressed, isolated from one another, and (ironically) more sedentary—sitting in our cars rather than moving our legs—while pushing several planetary boundaries deep into the danger zone. (For detailed sustainable mobility and transportation targets, see Appendix C.)

This chapter explores how to change how you move to reclaim your health and respect your environmental values while still enjoying mobility and adventure.

The Faster You Live, the Bigger Your Impact

Think about how you spend your Earth share for travel. When you walk, your impact stays well within safe boundaries. Your muscles use food energy, your feet leave a small footprint, and you move at the speed humans evolved to travel. You can cycle to cover more territory even more efficiently and quickly. But as you accelerate—from bicycle to car to airplane—your demands explode beyond your Earth share's capacities.

If you drive long distances every day in a conventional fuel-burning passenger vehicle, you're demanding miles of roads and acres of parking lots that bisect and pave over habitat, pounds of brake pads and tires that shed health-threatening particles, and gallons of fuel that emit global warming pollution.

The faster you live, the more planetary resources you're likely to consume. Driving is speedier than cycling but causes more transportation impacts. Flying is quicker than driving but causes even greater impacts. A jet-setting lifestyle costs our Earth dearly.

Strategies for Sustainable Movement

Along the movement pathway, three strategies keep your travel budget within your Earth share:

Reduce travel miles by living, working, and playing closer to home. You don't have to be a hermit—just establish a fulfilling life that doesn't require constant high-speed motion.

Get exercise while moving by walking and cycling for routine trips. Active transportation improves your physical and mental health, connects you with your community, and saves money. It's the rare solution that benefits your body as much as it benefits your planet.

Drive electric when you need to go farther or faster than your muscles allow. Electric vehicles are four or more times more efficient than fuel-burning ones and can run on electricity generated from sunshine. They're not perfect—better battery technology is still being developed—but they're a vast improvement over vehicles with combustion engines.

 ## High-Impact Movement Practices

Walk, Cycle, or Take Public Transit

Half of all trips in the United States are less than three miles—a distance easily covered by bicycle in 15 minutes or on foot in 45 minutes. Redirect your reflex to reach for car keys for every trip and rediscover the joy of getting around under your own power.

Walk to the grocery store instead of driving. Bicycle to the coffee shop. Take the bus to work. Each journey you make without starting an engine is a victory for your health and your planet. Get exercise without paying for gym time. Save money on fuel and parking. Notice things in your neighborhood you've been driving past for years and say hi to neighbors when you're walking or waiting for the bus.

Drive Electric Vehicles When You Can't Walk

Sometimes you need to go farther than your legs can carry you, take a trip during inclement weather that's hazardous for bicycling, or travel where public transit doesn't go. For these trips, electric vehicles are a sustainable choice. An EV charged anywhere on grid power in North America produces less pollution than a fuel-burning car—and that gap widens as grids go solar.

The real magic happens when you pair your EV with your own solar modules. Then you're driving on sunshine—your own energy ecosystem that operates for decades without drilling, refining, or burning anything more. Your Earth share can produce enough solar electricity to power all your local driving needs, leaving you with plenty of power to spare. If you'd rather not own a vehicle, you can choose electric when using ride-sharing services, rent an EV for longer trips, or advocate for electric buses in your community.

Your Sustainable Movement Dashboard

Use our online tools to track how your movement choices affect your Earth share, then decide whether you want to improve.

__Measuring Your Progress:__ At www.suspra.com you'll find optional online tools for evaluating your sustainability and personalizing guidance to your specific situation, all for free. To use a tool, you can type the link into a web browser or point your smart phone's camera at the box of dots for the QR code.

How fast is your lifestyle?	
Can you travel 27 miles or less per day on average? www.suspra.com/score/speed	 Speed

Seven Pathways to Sustainable Living

How do you get around?	
Can 50% of your trips be human-powered? Can 80% of your driving miles be electric? Can you limit flights to one per year or less? www.suspra.com/score/trips	

Toward Sustainable Movement Practices

Once you understand your current practices, you can take informed steps that will make the biggest positive difference. Here are practical steps at every level; for more, see *Sustainable Practices: Your Handbook for Effective Action*.

This Week: Quick-Start Actions

Walk One Errand. Walk, instead of driving, to do one errand this week—buying milk, mailing a letter, or returning a library book. Pay attention to the weather on your skin, sounds you'd miss sealed in a car, and neighborhood details you've never noticed. This isn't travel; it's presence.

Map Your Walkable World. On a mental map, draw a circle representing a 15-minute walk from your home. Mark every destination within that circle: friends, stores, restaurants, parks, and other services.

Plan One Car-Free Day. Pick a day not to use your car at all. Plan ahead: arrange any necessary trips for other days, organize activities close to home, or use the day to discover what's accessible without driving. Treat it as an experiment, not a sacrifice.

This Month: Building Better Habits

Track Your Mileage. Keep a simple log of your daily travel: how far you go and by what mode. Use your baseline data to set goals and track your progress toward achieving them.

Establish Active Transportation Routes. Identify three destinations you visit regularly—workplace, grocery store, gym—and figure out the best walking or cycling route to each. Explore routes on a day when you're not rushed. Learn where bike lanes are, which streets have good sidewalks, and where you can safely cross busy roads.

Invest in Proper Gear. Good walking shoes, a comfortable bicycle or tricycle, weather-appropriate clothing, and safety equipment make active transportation practical year-round. A quality rain jacket, bicycle lights, and a sturdy lock remove common barriers to walking and cycling. This one-time investment pays dividends for years.

Choose Electric When Ride-Sharing. When you hail a ride, select the electric option.

Try Multimodal Commuting. Combine transportation modes: drive to a park-and-ride, then take the bus downtown. Bicycle to the train station. Walk to a carpool pickup point.

This Year: Transformative Changes

Achieve Car-Light Living. Work toward days or weeks without using your personal vehicle. This might mean joining a car-sharing service for occasional needs, mastering your public transit system, or investing in an electric cargo bike or bike trailer for hauling groceries and gear. Make driving the exception rather than the rule.

Transition to Electric. If you need to own a vehicle, make your next one electric. Compare models, understand charging options, and calculate your total cost of owning or leasing before you buy.

Relocate Strategically. Living within walking distance of your daily needs is the single most sustainable transportation choice you can make. When life presents a natural transition point—new job, kids leaving home, lease ending—move to a more walkable neighborhood.

Lead Community Change. Advocate for better walking and cycling infrastructure in your community. Join or create a "Safe Routes to School" program. Organize "walking school buses" where parents take turns walking groups of children to school. Start a "Bike to Work" group at your office. Your leadership makes sustainable transportation easier for everyone.

Common Concerns and Solutions

"My area isn't walkable or bikeable." Start with what's possible, even if it's just walking up and down your street for exercise instead of driving to the gym. Advocate for pedestrian and cycling infrastructure—many communities have successfully transformed car-centric areas into people-friendly spaces. Consider an electric bicycle to extend your range and to handle hills with ease.

"Electric vehicles are too expensive." Buy a used EV. If buying isn't feasible, choose electric when using ride-sharing services or renting cars.

"Weather makes active transportation impractical." There's a common saying: "There's no bad weather, only bad gear." Invest in quality rain gear, warm layers, and appropriate footwear. Walking and cycling in weather you once thought impossible is invigorating and makes you feel capable and happy to be alive at a time when outdoor clothing and recreation technology allow you to experience new things.

"I need my car for work." Walk or bike for non-work trips, carpool with colleagues, or (if your job can be done remotely) negotiate with your boss to work from home.

"Public transit is inconvenient where I live." Try it just to see whether you can manage the inconvenience. Learn the routes, download the apps, and give yourself extra time to reach your destination. You may find that the chance to think or people-watch on the bus beats fighting traffic.

Your Movement Creates Your World

How you move through your life shapes our world itself. Every transportation choice you make affects your community. Walk and bike more, and you're reducing traffic. Take transit, and you're contributing to better service. Drive electric, and you're eliminating air pollution in your neighborhood.

Your Earth Share

Transportation isn't just about infrastructure—it's about life. When you walk your child to school, you share precious minutes holding hands and talking that would be lost in the rush of drop-off lanes. When you bicycle to work, you arrive energized rather than stressed out. When you take the bus, you meet and greet the driver, earning social capital one conversation at a time.

Your Earth share can easily support your transportation needs. Our challenge isn't technological—it's imagining what a good life looks like: knowing your neighborhood intimately because you walk it daily, being fit and healthy because you exercise on every errand and having more money to spend on other things besides pumping gas and maintaining your car.

Pathway #5: Energy
Powering Your Future

Our sun delivers more energy to our Earth in one hour than all of humanity uses in an entire year. Yet, most people remain tethered to fossil fuels—burning in minutes what formed deep underground over millions of years.

Natural gas can warm your living room—but results in dangerous methane leaks at every stage from wellhead to burner. Grid electricity from a coal power plant can illuminate a lamp—but leads miners to move mountains, literally. Solar power, harnessing a tiny bit of a massive natural energy flow from star to planet, can provide warmth, light, and everything else that energy from fossil fuel can deliver—and creates a sustainable system of modular energy-producing devices made from metal and glass that can be reused and recycled to provide energy forever.

A leaf captures sunlight and converts it into useful electricity without drilling, refining, or burning anything. Now imagine your home doing the same—harvesting the sunshine that reaches your property, storing what you need, sharing the excess with your community. This happens in millions of homes today. Yours can be next.

Your Energy Share of Earth's Balance

Did you know that the United States wastes two-thirds of its energy through the inefficiency of burning fuel? For every $100 we pay for energy, only $33 actually buys useful work. When we burn fuel for energy, physics limits us to capturing only about one-third of the energy released—the rest becomes waste heat. This isn't poor engineering; it's thermodynamics. Electric motors, however, can convert electricity to useful work at an efficiency of 90% or more, which is why *electrification* dramatically reduces energy consumption.

Ever wonder why fuel-burning cars need huge radiators to keep their engines cool, but electric vehicles don't? Most fuel-burning cars get less than 30 miles per gallon, while most EVs get over 100 miles per "gallon" of equivalent energy. Burning stuff produces more heat than motion, whereas controlling current is a cool way to move.

A typical suburban roof that gets full sun can generate enough solar electricity for an energy-efficient all-electric home. Combining efficiency, electrification, and solar adds up to a sustainable energy solution, but takes careful planning and financial management to achieve. (For detailed solar calculations, see Appendix A.)

Strategies for Sustainable Energy Use

Along the energy pathway, four strategies align your home with your sustainable Earth share energy budget:

Optimize energy efficiency by investing in technology and techniques that deliver the same comfort and convenience while using less energy. An LED bulb uses 80% less energy to provide the same amount of light as an incandescent bulb. A heat pump uses 75% less energy to deliver the same amount of warmth as a gas furnace. An EV uses 75% less energy to travel the same distance as a fuel-burning vehicle.

Conserve energy by consciously choosing to use less, accepting minor lifestyle adjustments for major planetary benefit. Lowering your thermostat by two degrees in winter, air-drying clothes in summer, and turning off lights when leaving a room all reduce demand without requiring any investment.

Electrify everything by replacing fuel-burning equipment with electric alternatives. You can replace every appliance that burns gas, oil, or propane in your home with a sustainably superior electric version—from your furnace to your stove to your water heater.

Solarize your power supply by generating or purchasing electricity from renewable sources. Whether through solar gadgets, plug-in balcony solar modules, rooftop or ground-mount arrays, community solar subscriptions, or choosing renewable energy from your utility, you can ensure your electric home runs on clean power.

 High-Impact Energy Practices

Seal and Insulate

Use caulk, foam, and other methods to keep conditioned air from leaking out through walls, ceilings, floors, and around doors. The average American home leaks so much air that it's equivalent to leaving a window open all the time. If you live in a climate that requires air conditioning or heating your home, these leaks probably waste more energy than all your appliances combined.

Start in your attic, where warm air naturally rises and escapes. Seal around light fixtures, plumbing vents, and the attic hatch. Add insulation to reach a resistance to heat flow of R-38 or higher. Move to your basement, sealing the rim joists where the foundation meets the wood framing—a few cans of spray foam can cut your heating bill by 20%. Install weatherstripping on doors and windows. These unglamorous improvements deliver a big return on investment.

Use LED Lighting

LED bulbs represent one of the greatest energy efficiency breakthroughs in recent history. Replacing an incandescent lamp with an LED will save megawatt-hours of electricity over its lifetime.

But don't stop at bulb replacement. Add occupancy sensors so lights turn off automatically. Install dimmer switches programmed to adjust based on available daylight. These smart controls can cut your lighting energy use by another half while extending lamp life even further.

Wash Clothes in Cold Water

If you wash your clothes in hot water, heating water accounts for most of the energy your laundering uses. Modern cold-water detergents with plant-based enzymes clean just as effectively as hot water—often better, since hot water can set stains and fade colors.

Upgrade to an ENERGY STAR-certified washer that uses less water and less energy than standard models and install a filter to trap microfibers.

Front-loaders extract more water during the spin cycle, reducing drying time and energy—a sustainability twofer.

Heat Water Using Electric Heat Pumps

Your water heater is likely your home's second-biggest energy user after space heating and cooling. A heat pump water heater works like a refrigerator in reverse, extracting heat from the surrounding air to warm your water. It is up to four times more energy-efficient than a gas-burning water heater and uses two-thirds less energy than a conventional electric water heater. Modern heat pump water heaters include smart controls that learn your usage patterns, heating water when electricity is cheapest and cleanest. They provide free air conditioning and dehumidification as a bonus.

Dry Clothes in a Condensing Dryer or on Racks

Conventional vented dryers blast heated air through wet clothes, blowing out heated or cooled air from your home and sucking in air from the outdoors. Ventless condensing dryers don't do that, using much less energy while being gentler on fabrics.

Better yet, a clothesline or drying rack allows evaporation to happen at a natural pace—faster in the sun on a windy day, slower in the shade on a calm day. Air-dried clothes last longer, smell fresher, and cost nothing to dry. In winter, indoor drying adds needed humidity to dry heated air. Modern drying racks fold flat for storage and roll out when needed.

Keep Food Cold in Energy-Efficient Refrigerators

That old 1970s-vintage refrigerator humming in your basement might be wasting hundreds or thousands of kilowatt-hours of electricity every year. Over just a couple of years, that costs more than a new, efficient model would cost to buy. Today's ENERGY STAR refrigerators use advanced insulation, variable-speed compressors, and precise temperature controls to minimize energy use.

When shopping, size matters: a too-large refrigerator wastes energy cooling empty space, whereas two smaller refrigerators use more energy than one larger one. Choose the smallest model that meets your needs. Position it away from heat sources like ovens and direct sunlight. Clean the coils twice yearly. These simple steps can cut refrigeration energy use by a quarter.

Cook with Induction and Convection

Induction cooktops use magnetic fields to heat pans directly, wasting much less cooking energy than technologies that heat up the air around cookware. Water boils in half the time of gas. Temperature responds instantly. The cooktop stays cool, preventing burns and making cleanup easy.

Convection ovens circulate hot air for faster, more even cooking at lower temperatures. Induction cooktops with convection ovens use half the energy that gas ranges and ovens require, while eliminating indoor air pollution from combustion and providing more precise control for better results every time.

Use Electric Heat Pumps for Space Heating

Heat pumps don't generate heat; they move it. In winter (even when it's freezing outside), they extract warmth from outdoor air and release it inside; modern cold-climate heat pumps work down to well below freezing. In summer, they reverse to provide air conditioning. Over a full heating or cooling season, they move three or four watts of heat for every watt of electricity consumed.

Compared to gas furnaces, heat pumps reduce heating costs while eliminating carbon monoxide risk and gas leak dangers. Paired with solar modules, they can heat your home using the sunlight that would otherwise simply bounce off your roof, driveway, or yard.

Go Solar

Solar modules have plummeted in cost over the past decade while becoming more efficient. An energy-efficient home in a sunny location can meet all of its energy needs from the sunlight that reaches it. Go solar to convert your home from an energy liability depleting Earth's fossil reserves into a power asset harvesting solar abundance. With battery storage, you gain energy independence and blackout protection.

Your Earth Share

Can't install solar on your property? Subscribe to a community solar farm that feeds clean power to the grid on your behalf.

Your Sustainable Energy Dashboard

Use our online tools to track your progress toward sustainable energy independence with these key metrics.

> ***Measuring Your Progress:*** *At www.suspra.com you'll find optional online tools for evaluating your sustainability and personalizing guidance to your specific situation, all for free. To use a tool, you can type the link into a web browser or point your smart phone's camera at the box of dots for the QR code.*

How much power do you need?
Can you meet your needs using 0.8 kW or less per person?   www.suspra.com/score/power

What percentage of your energy is electricity versus fuel?
Can you reach 100% electric for all home energy?   www.suspra.com/score/electricity

Seven Pathways to Sustainable Living

How much of your energy is solar?	
Can you achieve 100% solar electricity? www.suspra.com/score/solar	

Toward Sustainable Energy Practices

Once you understand your home's energy profile, you can prioritize upgrades that deliver the biggest impact for your investment. Here's a practical roadmap, drawing from dozens of practices described in *Sustainable Practices: Your Handbook for Effective Action*:

This Week: Quick-Start Actions

Seal Obvious Leaks. Walk around with a lit incense stick on a cold and windy day—smoke movement reveals air leaks. Seal them with caulk or weatherstripping. Focus on windows, doors, and electrical outlets on exterior walls. This is a great project for a weekend of miserable weather.

Replace Five Bulbs. Start with your most-used lights—kitchen, living room, porch—and then continue to replace lighting as older bulbs burn out. LED lamps and fixtures are now the standard and widely available. Read the packaging to understand lighting terms that may be new to you, such as lumens and color temperature, in addition to wattage (power consumption).

Adjust Your Thermostat. For every two degrees lower in winter, and higher in summer (if you have air conditioning), you set your thermostat, you'll save somewhere between 5% and 10% on heating and cooling. Program setbacks to save even more without sacrificing comfort.

Wash in Cold. Switch your washing machine from hot to cold water. Your clothes will last longer, colors stay brighter, and you'll save energy.

This Month: Building Better Habits

Schedule an Energy Audit. Many utilities offer free or subsidized professional energy audits that identify your biggest energy waste. An auditor will use infrared cameras to find hidden leaks and test your insulation levels. The audit report becomes your upgrade roadmap.

Install Smarter Controls. Add smart power strips that eliminate phantom loads from devices in standby mode. Install a programmable thermostat, if you don't have one, or a better programmable thermostat, if you don't use the one you have now.

Research Heat Pumps. If you're still burning fuel to heat your home, get quotes for replacing your furnace or air conditioner with a heat pump. Even if you're not ready to buy now, understanding your options prepares you for when your current system needs replacement.

Compare Solar Options. Research local solar installers and community solar programs. Ask for a free assessment showing your potential savings–reputable companies will be happy to provide one. This will help you make an informed decision when you're ready to go solar.

This Year: Transformative Changes

Complete Your Envelope Upgrade. Bring your home's insulation up to modern standards in your attic, walls, and floors over unconditioned spaces. Combined with air sealing, insulation can cut cooling and heating energy use in half.

Electrify Major Appliances. As gas appliances need replacement, choose electric alternatives. The big ones are your furnace, water heater, clothes dryer, and cooktop and oven. Each conversion prepares your home to become fossil-fuel-free and 100% solar powered.

Install Solar + Storage. Add solar arrays with battery backup to generate and store your own electricity. You'll lock in an energy supply for decades while increasing your home's value.

Achieve Energy Independence. Through efficiency, electrification, and solarization, produce as much energy as you consume annually.

Thousands of ordinary families have achieved complete energy independence, proving it's possible with today's technology.

Common Concerns and Solutions

"Heat pumps don't work in cold climates." Modern cold-climate heat pumps work at outdoor temperatures as low as -15°F (-26°C). Maine—not exactly tropical—is leading the nation in heat pump adoption because they work so well. If you live in an area with cold winters, specify cold-climate models with variable-speed compressors.

"Solar is too expensive." Solar costs dropped 90% between 2015 and 2025. A good financing package will make a project cash-flow positive from day one. If you can't or don't want to install solar on your own property, community solar (i.e., paying for grid power that a remote solar array generates) requires zero upfront cost and may cost less than conventional electricity.

"My utility rates are too low to justify upgrades." What value do you place on environmental benefits?

"I rent and can't make major changes." Focus on what you can control: LED bulbs, smart power strips, cold-water washing, portable induction cooktops, plug-in solar modules. Ask your landlord about upgrades that increase property value. See if your utility offers programs specifically for renters.

"Our electrical panel needs upgrading." Start with energy-efficient upgrades that use less power: you can always screw in a light bulb or plug in an appliance that uses fewer watts than the one it replaces. When a panel upgrade is necessary, it's a one-time investment that prepares your home for your all-electric future.

Your Energy Transformation

The sun rises every morning, sending more than enough energy for everyone on Earth. The technology to harvest is already affordable and continues to improve every year. Your Earth share includes enough solar energy to power a comfortable, modern life forever. The only question is when you'll make the switch from depleting fossil reserves to harvesting renewable flows.

Energy isn't just about kilowatts and carbon pollution—it's about the kind of future we're powering. Every efficiency upgrade you make, every gallon of heating oil you don't burn, every kilowatt-hour of solar electricity you generate is a step toward a world powered by endless abundance rather than shackled to hopeless depletion.

Your home can be part of Earth's natural energy flow, harvesting the sunshine that reaches your roof, using it efficiently, and sharing the excess with your community. You'll save money, gain energy independence, and create a healthier indoor environment. But beyond these personal benefits, you'll demonstrate that sustainable energy isn't a sacrifice—it's an upgrade.

So seal that drafty window. Replace those old bulbs. Turn down your water heater. Sign up for community solar. Each action builds momentum toward bigger changes and more clean power for all.

Pathway #6: Goods

Turning the Circular Economy

Many of your material possessions will outlive you—they may change shape and form, but somewhere on Earth, the materials of your possessions will persist. That smartphone in your pocket, those shoes in your closet, the plastic wrapper from this morning's breakfast—your material goods are on a journey that extends far beyond your ownership and use.

Nature operates in cycles. A leaf falls, decomposes, feeds the soil, nourishes new growth to create a new leaf. No waste, no landfills, no floating garbage patches. But for manufactured items we've created a different system—a slide from extraction to disposal, from mine to dump, from oil well to ocean gyre. Every year, humanity extracts billions of tons of materials from Earth and then burns or buries them in landfills rather than reusing or recycling them.

When materials flow in regenerative cycles rather than one-way trips to the dump, the limiting factor in how much "stuff" you can use is how much solar energy is available to transport and recycle it. Your Earth share can sustainably provide you with about 55 pounds (25 kilograms) of materials per day—enough for a comfortable life. Unfortunately, the average American consumes twice that amount, including products designed to be thrown "away" after a single use. But there is no "away"—just places we've agreed to pile our discards until someone else figures out what to do with them.

This chapter explores how to transform your relationship with material goods from a wasteful slide to a regenerative cycle.

Your Material Share of Earth's Abundance

If you demand too many material goods per year, you push your Earth share beyond its limits. Mining for new metal and coal destroys habitats and pollutes watersheds. Extracting oil and gas depletes reserves.

Manufacturing plastics drives climate change and leaks novel chemicals into groundwater. Ocean plastic threatens marine ecosystems. Every bit of stuff you buy changes some part of our planet.

Reducing the mass of goods you consume gives your sustainable share of Earth a chance to catch up with your demands. Once you've minimized your rate of consumption, you can help your Earth share continue to meet your needs by thoughtfully considering the type of materials you buy. For example, metal can be recycled over and over without having to mine for more, but virgin plastic can only be made once. If you use plastic instead of metal, you contribute to the problems of coal mining, petroleum drilling, and fracking, because plastic is made from coal, oil, and gas.

Strategies for Sustainable Material Flows

Along the goods pathway, four interconnected strategies align your consumption with your Earth share's regenerative capacity:

Economize consumption by buying less stuff, choosing quality over quantity, and resisting the constant pressure to purchase. The greenest goods are the ones you don't buy.

Choose eco-friendly goods made from renewable, non-toxic materials that can be completely composted or recycled. Wood, glass, and metal can be recycled well.

Maintain and reuse everything possible, extending product lifespans through care, repair, and creative repurposing. Maintaining an item to last 20 years is usually a better idea than not maintaining it and having to replace it every two years.

Manage waste wisely by composting organic materials and recycling metals, glass, and clean cardboard while avoiding materials that must be buried or burned for disposal.

 High-Impact Goods Practices

Compost Biodegradable Solid Waste

Composting is alchemy—transforming waste into wealth for the soil. Those banana peels, coffee grounds, and autumn leaves aren't garbage. They're nutrients, temporarily borrowed from soil, that yearn to return. When you compost, you're closing a loop that industrial agriculture broke, returning organic matter to build healthy soil instead of generating methane in landfills.

You can start simple in a corner of your yard with a pile of leaves mixed with kitchen scraps, allowing natural decomposition to do the work. No fancy equipment required—Earth composted for billions of years before humans invented tumblers and thermometers. In apartments, a small worm bin or countertop composter can handle food scraps. Many cities now offer curbside composting, making it as easy as recycling.

Composting fundamentally changes how you see waste. That apple core is future soil. That cardboard box is carbon to balance nitrogen in your compost. Once you start composting, you'll find yourself naturally avoiding products with non-compostable packaging, creating a positive feedback loop toward sustainability.

Recycle Metal, Cardboard, and Glass; Avoid Plastic

Recycling works brilliantly for some materials and fails miserably for others. Aluminum cans become new cans endlessly, with 95% less energy than making new aluminum. Glass bottles melt into new bottles forever. Clean cardboard efficiently becomes new cardboard. These materials have genuine circular potential.

But plastic recycling is mostly a myth. Of all plastic ever made, less than 10% has been recycled even once. Why? Because "plastic" isn't one material—it's thousands of different polymers. That recycling symbol with a number? It's not a guarantee of recyclability; it's just an identification code of general category. Most plastic gets "downcycled" into lower-grade products once, then landfilled or burned.

The sustainable solution to plastic is to stop buying it. Choose products in aluminum, glass, or cardboard packaging. Buy in bulk using your own containers. Select durable goods made from materials that last. When you must buy plastic, choose products made from single categories (all polyethylene terephthalate plastic #1, all high-density polyethylene plastic #2, or all polypropylene plastic #5) rather than mixed plastic types that can't be recycled cost-effectively.

Your Sustainable Goods Dashboard

Monitor how materials flow through your life and where they go when you're done with them. Use our online tools to track how you're doing now and plan how to achieve your future goals.

> ***Measuring Your Progress:*** *At www.suspra.com you'll find optional online tools for evaluating your sustainability and personalizing guidance to your specific situation, all for free. To use a tool, you can type the link into a web browser or point your smart phone's camera at the box of dots for the QR code.*

How much stuff do you buy?	
Can you keep purchases under 55 pounds per person per day? www.suspra.com/score/consumption	 Consumption

Seven Pathways to Sustainable Living

What materials do you choose?	
Can 80% of your purchases be non-toxic and recyclable? Can you eliminate single-use plastics? www.suspra.com/score/materials	

How well do you close the loop?	
Can you compost 100% of your organic waste? Can you recycle 100% of the metal, glass, and clean cardboard you use? Can you divert 100% of your hazardous materials from landfills? www.suspra.com/score/circularity	

Toward Sustainable Goods Practices

Once you understand what's flowing through your home, you can make strategic changes that dramatically improve your sustainable goods score. Here are practical steps; for more comprehensive guidance, see *Sustainable Practices: Your Handbook for Effective Action*.

This Week: Quick-Start Actions

Conduct a Plastic Audit. Count every piece of single-use plastic you discard this week. Don't judge, just observe. Note which items could be eliminated (single-use plastic shopping bags with reusable bags), which could be replaced (plastic wrap with beeswax wraps), and which seem unavoidable (medication packaging). Awareness precedes change.

Set Up Proper Sorting. Create clearly labeled stations for compost, recycling, landfill, and hazardous materials. Learn your local recycling rules—they vary widely. Download your community's recycling app or print its guidelines. Make correct sorting almost as easy as tossing everything in one bin.

Switch Three Products. Replace three disposable items with reusable alternatives: cloth napkins for paper, rechargeable batteries for disposables, and a refillable water bottle for plastic bottles. Start with changes that feel easy. Success builds momentum.

Resist One Purchase. When tempted to buy something this week, wait 48 hours. Often, the urge passes. If you still want it, check if you can borrow, rent, or buy used instead. Every purchase avoided is a victory for your Earth share.

This Month: Building Better Habits

Join the Sharing Economy. Sign up for your local Buy Nothing group, Freecycle network, or neighborhood swap. Offer things you don't need; request things you do. Join a tool library or start informal sharing with neighbors. Most people use a drill only a few times per year—everyone on your block doesn't need to own one.

Master Maintenance. Read the care instructions for items you want to last—appliances, tools, clothes, furniture. Follow the maintenance schedules. Clean refrigerator coils, oil wooden furniture, sharpen knives, and wash filters. Proper care can double or triple product lifespans.

Buy Concentrates and Bulk. Switch to concentrated cleaners, detergents, and soaps that you dilute at home. Shop with reusable bags and containers at bulk bins. A single bottle of concentrate can replace dozens of ready-to-use bottles. Bulk buying eliminates mountains of packaging.

Create a Repair Kit. Assemble basic repair supplies: needle and thread, super glue, duct tape, screwdrivers, and patches. Learn one simple repair—sewing a button, patching a hole, gluing a broken handle. YouTube University offers free repair education for almost anything.

This Year: Transformative Changes

Achieve a Zero Waste Bathroom. Transform your bathroom into a zero-waste zone with bar soaps and shampoos that come in recyclable cardboard instead of plastic bottles, bamboo toothbrushes, and other hygiene products made from natural materials that you can compost.

Build Community Systems. Organize a neighborhood repair café where people fix things together monthly. Start a community compost system for those without yard space. Create a local "library of things" for rarely-used items like carpet cleaners, tile saws, and camping gear.

Shift to Conscious Consumption. Before any purchase, ask: Do I need this or want it? Could I borrow or rent instead? Will I use it enough to justify its environmental cost? Can I buy it used? Is it repairable? What will happen to it when I'm done with it?

Flat Out Refuse Waste. Refuse single-use anything. Choose products with no packaging or packaging you can return to the vendor. Buy nothing that can't be composted, truly recycled, or used for decades. Support companies designing products for disassembly and material recovery.

Common Concerns and Solutions

"Eco-friendly products cost too much." Buy quality used items for the price of cheap new ones. Plan a 36-month budget and eliminate disposable products to save money over time.

"My area doesn't have good recycling." Focus on the top of the waste hierarchy: refuse, reduce, reuse. Buy less. Compost at home to divert organic waste. Save recyclables for trips to areas with better recycling facilities.

"My family resists changes." Start with invisible swaps—concentrated detergents, rechargeable batteries, cloth napkins that feel nicer than paper. Make sustainable choices more convenient than wasteful ones. Celebrate wins like money saved or reduced trash volume. Change household systems in ways that make it easier to do the right thing.

"Everything is packaged in plastic." Shop farmers markets with reusable bags. Choose stores with bulk bins. Buy from companies committed to plastic-free packaging. When plastic is unavoidable, choose products in #1 polyethylene terephthalate (PETE) or #2 high-density polyethylene (HDPE) plastics.

"Things aren't made to last anymore." True, but quality items still exist. Research before buying. Select products that are designed for repair or recycling.

Today's Choices Create Tomorrow's World

Every purchase is a push toward the world you want. Buy disposable, and you're demanding more extraction, manufacturing, and landfilling. Buy durable, repairable, and recyclable, and you're encouraging a circular economy that works within planetary boundaries.

The goods flowing through your life represent embodied energy, embedded water, and transformed ecosystems. That plastic bag is actually ancient organisms, exposed to extreme heat and pressure over millions of years, extracted, refined, manufactured, and shipped—all for a few minutes of use. Understanding these histories transforms how you view everyday objects.

But this isn't about nostalgia. It's about next steps—making your material choices reflect your values. Compost those coffee grounds. Fix that broken zipper. Share that tool you rarely use. Each action, however small, helps reshape our economy from a straight line from extraction to single-use to landfill into a regenerative circle of reuse, recycle, and respect.

Pathway #7: Habitat

Creating Space for Nature

A robin building her nest doesn't clear-cut a forest to make room for her family. Instead, she weaves her shelter into a tree, using materials the ecosystem provides, creating a home that will eventually return to the soil, nourishing the very tree that supported it. Her instinct teaches that a home isn't something we take from nature—it's something we create within it.

Every square foot you control—your room, your house, your yard—is simultaneously human habitat and potential miniature wildlife sanctuary. You can't decide whether your home will affect the broader ecosystem (it will), but you can choose to enhance or diminish the web of life surrounding it. When you choose native shrubs over lawn, permeable surfaces over concrete, or organic methods over synthetic chemicals, you're stewarding your patch of Earth's living surface.

That native flower in a pot on your windowsill can harbor caterpillars that become butterflies that pollinate your neighbor's vegetables. The rain garden you install prevents flooding downstream while recharging groundwater for everyone. The organic methods you use to manage pests protect the soil organisms that keep all plants healthy. You're not just a renter or a homeowner—you're a habitat manager whose decisions affect countless other lives.

Your Share of Earth's Habitat

Remember, if Earth were divided equally among all humans, your share of habitable land is about the size of a soccer field, give or take. Do you want to build over and mow your whole field? The less land you alter for your shelter and surroundings, the more you can make available for the ecosystems that sustain us all.

The average American single-family detached home occupies about 2,500 square feet of a quarter-acre lot. That leaves roughly 8,000 square feet of potential natural habitat. Multiply that by millions of homes, and suburban yards become a vast, distributed nature preserve that we could build. Will you manage your yard as a sterile outdoor carpet or as an integral part of a continental-scale system for biodiversity?

Strategies for Sustainable Habitat

Along the habitat pathway, three interconnected strategies align your property management with ecological health:

Choose sustainable shelter by living in an appropriately-sized, well-located home that minimizes habitat disruption. Sharing walls, choosing infill development over sprawl, and right-sizing your living space all reduce the total human footprint on the landscape. Green building certifications ensure your shelter meets high environmental standards.

Renovate wisely using non-toxic materials and techniques that improve rather than degrade your indoor and outdoor environment. Every renovation is an opportunity to remove hazards like lead paint and asbestos, increase occupancy to house more people in existing structures, and upgrade to healthier materials that don't off-gas toxic chemicals.

Protect natural systems by managing your landscape to support rather than suppress ecological processes. Native plants, organic maintenance, permeable surfaces, and wild areas all help your property function as part of nature rather than apart from it.

 A High-Impact Habitat Practice

Landscape with Native Plants Organically

That sea of perfect lawn might look tidy, but ecologically, it's a catastrophe. Native plants that evolved in your region over thousands of years support hundreds of species of insects, birds, and other wildlife. Easy-to-mow grass, kept short and free of "weeds," does not.

Learn what naturally grows in your region; check with your state's native plant society. Replace a section of lawn or a non-native shrub with native alternatives. Watch what happens: butterflies appear, birds visit more frequently, and the soil becomes richer. Native plants, adapted to local rainfall, soil, and pests, typically need less water and no fertilizer or pesticides once established.

Pair native plants with organic methods: apply compost instead of synthetic chemical fertilizer, release beneficial insects instead of pesticides, and use mulch instead of herbicides. You're not just avoiding chemicals—you're building a resilient ecosystem that maintains its own health. Your yard becomes a refuge for struggling pollinators, a corridor for wildlife movement, and a classroom where children don't have to drive to visit nature—it's right outside your door.

Your Sustainable Habitat Dashboard

Track how your property management affects the broader web of life. Use our online tools to see how you're doing and how you can improve.

> ***Measuring Your Progress:*** *At www.suspra.com you'll find optional online tools for evaluating your sustainability and personalizing guidance to your specific situation, all for free. To use a tool, you can type the link into a web browser or point your smart phone's camera at the box of dots for the QR code.*

How densely do you live?	
How many people per thousand square feet does your property house? www.suspra.com/score/occupancy	

Your Earth Share

What green building standards do you meet?	
Does your home have any green certifications? Have you eliminated toxins like lead and asbestos? www.suspra.com/score/building	 Building

How much habitat do you protect?	
What percentage of your property supports native species? Do you donate to land conservation? www.suspra.com/score/conservation	 Conservation

How do you manage your landscape?	
Can you eliminate synthetic pesticides and fertilizers? Can 50% of your landscape be native plants? www.suspra.com/score/landscape	 Landscape

Toward Sustainable Habitat Practices

Once you understand your property's ecological potential, you can take steps to help it flourish as both human shelter and wildlife habitat. Here are practical actions at every level; for more comprehensive guidance, see *Sustainable Practices: Your Handbook for Effective Action*.

This Week: Quick-Start Actions

Identify Your Natives. Walk your property with a plant identification app, field guide, or knowledgeable friend. Learn which native plants are still hanging on and which troublesome foreign species have been introduced. Knowledge informs action—you can better protect what you understand and recognize.

Keep a Wildlife List. Begin documenting the birds, butterflies, bees, and all other wildlife (no matter how tiny) you can find on your property. Bring a cellphone to take pictures. This baseline enables you to know whether your habitat improvements are working. Children love this activity—going outside becomes a research safari.

Choose a Chemical to Eliminate. Pick a synthetic lawn or garden chemical you've used and research organic alternatives. Those aphids on your roses? A spray of soapy water breaks down the aphids' waxy coating, dehydrating and killing them, without poisoning beneficial insects.

Create Space for the Wild Things. Designate one corner of your yard as a "no-mow, no-go, no-spray" zone. Let it grow wild and undisturbed. This tiny refuge provides cover for ground-nesting birds, overwintering sites for beneficial insects, and seeds for wildlife food.

This Month: Building Better Habits

Plant Your Next Native. Research native plants for your region through your state's native plant society or cooperative extension. Start with one easy species—perhaps a native shrub that provides berries for birds or a native perennial that feeds specialist pollinators. Plant it properly, water it well until it gets its root system established and see if it thrives without chemicals.

Build a Brush Pile. Instead of hauling branches to the curb, stack them on your soil in an out-of-the-way spot. This simple shelter can harbor a wide range of interesting species while the wood slowly decomposes to enrich your soil.

Switch to Organic Lawn Care. If you maintain lawn areas, transition to organic methods. Leave grass clippings to decompose (free nitrogen!), set your mower height to 3 inches (deeper roots, less water needed), and overseed with clover to naturally fertilize. Your lawn might not look like a golf course, but it will be safe for children and pets.

Install a Bird Bath. Provide clean water at pedestal height for birds. This simple feature can triple the bird species visiting your yard. Add a small solar fountain or change the water every few days to prevent mosquitoes—moving water makes it harder for them to lay their eggs.

This Year: Transformative Changes

Convert Lawn to Native Habitat. Transform at least half your lawn into native plant gardens, meadows, or food forests. Sheet mulch to smother grass without chemicals, then plant densely with native species. Group plants by water needs. Include layers—groundcovers, perennials, shrubs, and trees—to create a diverse habitat structure.

Achieve Habitat Certification. Meet the criteria for the National Wildlife Federation's Certified Wildlife Habitat, Homegrown National Park, or similar programs. These programs require food sources, water, cover, and places to raise young, plus sustainable practices. The certification sign you display educates neighbors and might inspire them to follow suit.

Install Green Infrastructure. Replace impermeable surfaces (such as asphalt or concrete) with permeable pavers, install rain gardens to manage stormwater, or create a green roof on sheds or garages. These features reduce flooding, recharge groundwater, and provide additional habitat while managing water sustainably on your property.

Remove Invasive Species. Learn to identify and remove invasive introduced plants that crowd out natives. This isn't a one-time job—invasives require persistent management—but removing them makes room for plants that are better able to serve a functional role in your local ecosystem, having co-evolved with all the species that interact to create a healthy environment over thousands of years.

Common Concerns and Solutions

"My HOA requires a traditional lawn." Some states now prohibit homeowner associations from banning native plants—check your local laws. Document the environmental and economic benefits of native landscaping. Many HOAs have updated rules after residents have started a demonstration garden, maintained it beautifully to show natives aren't "messy," and proposed a pilot program.

"Native plants look wild and unkempt." Design matters: signal intention with a crisp edge between native beds and paths. Use traditional design principles—repetition, structure, defined edges—with native plants. Include some native cultivars (nativars) that have tidier forms. Add well-marked paths and benches to show the space is cared for and intentionally managed.

"I rent and can't make major changes." Focus on containers and temporary improvements. Grow native plants in pots, provide water sources, hang bird feeders, and use organic methods for any maintenance you do. Talk to your landlord about improvements that increase property value—native landscaping reduces maintenance costs long-term.

"Wildlife might become pests." Design thoughtfully to encourage beneficial wildlife while discouraging problems. Place bird feeders away from windows, use native plants that don't produce messy fruits near walkways, and never directly feed mammals like mice, chipmunks, squirrels, or raccoons.

"I don't know anything about plants." Make an acquaintance with a plant species that strikes your fancy. Every expert began as a beginner. Join local native plant groups for free advice and plant swaps. See if there is a Master Gardener program offering free education in your town. Garden centers increasingly stock natives with good signage. You don't need to know everything—just be willing to learn.

Your Habitat Makes the World Whole

Every property decision you make either adds to or subtracts from Earth's capacity to support life. When you choose dense, efficient housing, you leave more room for nature. When you eliminate synthetic chemicals, you protect the soil organisms that sustain all terrestrial life. When you plant natives, you weave your property back into the ecosystem that existed long before suburbs.

Your yard might seem insignificant compared to vast forests and prairies, but collectively, suburban landscapes cover millions of acres. If every homeowner converted half their lawn to native habitat, we'd create the world's largest wildlife corridor. If every gardener went organic, we'd eliminate tons of toxic runoff. If every renovation used non-toxic materials, we'd dramatically improve indoor and outdoor air quality.

But beyond these collective impacts, managing your habitat sustainably changes you. You'll begin to notice the seasons through bird migrations and bloom times. You'll watch "your" butterflies complete their life cycles on plants you provided for them. You'll teach children that humans can live better with nature, not apart from it. Your property will become not just a shelter, but a sanctuary—for you and countless other lives.

Plant one native. Skip one chemical application. Let one corner grow wild. Watch what happens when you work with nature instead of against it. Your habitat is waiting to heal and be healed, to shelter and be sheltered, to become the living landscape it strives to be.

Seven Pathways to Sustainable Living

Measuring and Planning Next Steps

You've explored seven pathways to sustainability. You've learned twenty pivotal practices that can transform your environmental impact. What do you do next? How do you know if you're making real progress? What is a wise plan given your unique situation?

In this chapter, you'll learn how to assess where you are now, set priorities that match your resources and values, track meaningful progress, and create a resilient plan that builds momentum rather than frustration. Most importantly, you'll discover how to make sustainability a journey your whole household embraces rather than a solo crusade.

Your Sustainability Dashboard

Practicing sustainability means making wise choices with the resources your share of our planet can provide every day and respecting the processes that support all life on Earth. Every practice you've learned helps you live well within those boundaries. But with seven pathways and dozens of possible actions, it helps to see the whole picture—to understand how your environmental impacts add up.

That's where your *Suspra Score* comes in. Think of it as your environmental credit score, but instead of measuring how well you manage your finances, it measures how well you manage your quantifiable impacts on Earth's life support systems. A negative score means you're taking more from our planet than your Earth share can provide–you're making it harder for everyone else to survive. A positive score means you're on the sustainable side of the ledger, meeting your needs in ways that preserve and enhance Earth's capacity to meet everyone else's needs too.

Understanding Your Suspra Score

Your Suspra Score integrates sub-scores for each of the seven pathways.

Your Earth Share

Sub-Score	Indicates
Community	• Sustainability knowledge *Can you explain why your practices matter?* • Demonstrated practices *What are you actually doing?* • Social interaction *Are you helping others learn and act wisely?*
Food	• Food waste rate *How much of the food you procure do you eat?* • Beverage choices *What do you drink?* • Diet composition *What do you eat?* • Food sourcing *How is your food and drink produced?*
Water	• Water consumption rate *How much water do you use daily?* • Water quality protection *Are you polluting your local waters?*
Movement	• Average speed *How far do you travel daily?* • Transportation modes *How do you get around?*
Energy	• Average power *How much energy do you use daily?* • Electrification *How close are you to being 100% electric?* • Solar energy *How close are you to being 100% solar?*
Goods	• Material consumption rate *How much stuff do you consume daily?* • Material choices *How well are you choosing safe and sustainable materials?* • Waste management *How well are you diverting, composting, and recycling?*

Sub-Score	Indicates
Habitat	• Housing density *How many people can live in your housing?* • Sustainability certifications *How "green" are your buildings and property?* • Chemical use in landscaping *Are you polluting your local ecosystem?* • Native plants *Are you directly protecting natural habitat?* • Conservation support *Are you indirectly protecting natural habitat?*

Each pathway sub-score feeds into your overall Suspra Score. Remember, you don't need to be perfect. A sustainable future doesn't require eight billion environmental saints. It only needs enough of us making wise choices that, collectively, keep us on the safe side of planetary boundaries.

Measuring Where You Are

Before you take your next step on your sustainability journey, it might help to know where you're starting from and how far you want to go. Gathering this knowledge is the reason to calculate your Suspra Score. This isn't about judgment—it's about data. You can't manage what you don't measure. (For scoring details, benchmarks, and milestones, see Appendix C.)

Three Levels of Assessment

When you're ready to calculate a sustainability score for your household, our web app at www.suspra.com/score offers three levels of detail.

Quick Start (30 minutes): Spend a few minutes answering basic questions off the top of your head about your current practices. You'll get a rough baseline and ideas for improvement. This is perfect for getting started without getting bogged down in data collection.

Regular (2 hours): When you're ready to invest a little more time to calculate a score grounded in fact, not speculation, gather one year of utility bills, review your purchasing patterns, and answer questions with these facts in hand. This enables our web app to provide personalized recommendations based on real data, not just your best guesses.

Detailed (ongoing): To reveal seasonal patterns and measure your progress in the finest resolution, track your consumption and practices on an ongoing basis using the full array of tools available. This is best if you need evidence that you are achieving meaningful sustainability goals or want to fine tune your practices based on real-world feedback.

Your First Assessment

A Quick Start assessment gets you going—a rough idea is better than no idea. You won't know the answer to every question, but that's okay. Just give it your best guess.

If you're not satisfied with guessing, do a Regular assessment based on real data. For that, you'll need:

- A month's utility bills (electricity, gas, water)
- Vehicle mileage and records of flights you've taken
- Credit card or bank statements to determine your food budget and purchasing habits
- Logs of household practices

Your first assessment establishes a baseline. Then, when you take action to improve your practices, you can compare against this baseline to see how well your steps are achieving positive results.

Interpreting Your Results

Your initial scores might surprise you. Maybe you're doing better than expected in some areas (perhaps you rarely fly, giving you a great movement score) while lagging in others (maybe that old refrigerator in the basement is killing your energy score).

After you've calculated your score, our web app will share insights:

- **Quick wins**: Where small changes can yield big improvements

- **Hidden impacts**: Which practices are having the biggest impact on your score
- **Existing strengths**: Where you are already very sustainable
- **Structural challenges**: Which impacts will require major changes to improve

How to Take Your Next Steps

With your baseline established, you're ready to take steps and see how far they take you toward your sustainability goals.

The Power of Sequential Success

Attempting too many changes at once makes it harder to follow through. A better approach is to build momentum through many small successes—introduce one change at a time in a sequence that makes sense for your family.

Month 1-3: Start Good Habits. Pick three high-impact practices you can try with minimal cost or effort. Here are some ideas:

- Switch to cold water washing (saves energy)
- Prepare a plant-based meal once a week (reduces diet impact)
- Start composting food scraps (diverts waste, builds awareness)

Immediately establish sustainability as part of your living routines.

Month 4-6: Upgrade Systems. With habits established, tackle one significant upgrade:

- Install water-efficient fixtures throughout your home
- Install LED bulbs in lights you use a lot
- Find and seal air leaks in your attic and basement

Choose changes based on your first assessment results—take all your quick wins. A month or two later, calculate a Regular score using real data to see if you've made a positive difference that you can measure.

Month 7-12: Plan Investments, Research and plan for major improvements:

- Get quotes for solar panels or heat pumps

- Test drive electric vehicles
- Design native landscaping

Even if you won't make a major purchase immediately, understanding costs and benefits helps you save strategically and seize opportunities (like rebate programs or sales). Be prepared for the day when your heating system or vehicle needs to be replaced–do your research ahead of time. Don't keep putting it off, or you may be forced to make an important decision under time pressure.

Choosing Your Priorities

How do you choose what to do first? Consider four factors:

1. **Environmental Impact**: How much will this improve your Suspra Score?
2. **Dollar Value:** What's the return on investment? Free changes (like taking shorter showers) obviously beat expensive ones initially, but big investments often pay large returns over time.
3. **Difficulty**: How much effort does this require? Be honest about your capacity. You might find meal planning harder than installing LED bulbs. Do what you can, when you can.
4. **Readiness**: What is your household prepared to embrace? Start with changes that excite rather than threaten family members.

Financial Planning

"I can't afford to be sustainable" might be the most common misconception. In reality, many sustainable practices save money immediately, while others pay for themselves over time. "I can't afford to be *un*sustainable" is more often the truth.

Three Financial Strategies

Which financial strategy for sustainability works best for you depends on your situation.

Seven Pathways to Sustainable Living

1. **Resource Conservation (Save Now)**: Reduce consumption, accepting minor lifestyle adjustments for immediate savings (values are estimates; your actual savings may vary):
   - Shorter showers (save $100/year)
   - Eliminate food waste (save $1,500/year)
   - Walk instead of drive for short trips (save $500/year)
   - Drink tap water (save $800/year)

   Total potential: $3,000 annually with zero upfront cost

2. **Resource Efficiency (Invest Now to Save Later)**: Upgrade to efficient technology that pays for itself:
   - LED lighting throughout: invest $200 to save $400/year
   - Low-flow fixtures: invest $100 to save $100/year
   - Programmable thermostat: invest $200 to save $180/year
   - ENERGY STAR refrigerator: invest $1,000 to save $150/year

3. **Property Transformation (Invest for Environmental Impact)**: Major upgrades that dramatically reduce environmental impact:
   - Heat pump system: invest $10,000 to save $1,200/year
   - Solar panels: invest $15,000 to save $1,500/year
   - Electric vehicle: invest $35,000 to save $2,000/year

Finding Financial Resources

You may be able to leverage additional resources to achieve your goals.

Utility Rebates: Most utilities offer rebates for efficient appliances, insulation, and solar installations. Check www.dsireusa.org for programs in your area.

Tax Deductions and Credits: Politicians are constantly tweaking our tax codes. When you file your taxes, make sure you're claiming all the deductions and getting all the credits you are entitled to.

Financing Options: Work with financial professionals to borrow money to save money over the long run:

- PACE financing (property-assessed clean energy)
- Solar loans and leases
- Utility on-bill financing
- Green home improvement loans

Creative Funding:

- Group buys with neighbors for better pricing
- DIY installations where safe and legal
- Buying quality used items instead of new ones
- Bartering skills with friends

Creating Your Sustainability Budget

Consider better sustainability as a financial investment. Prime your cash flow pump by starting with practices that conserve resources and reduce your monthly expenses.

1. **Calculate current waste**: Add up what you spend on uneaten food, excess energy, wasted water, and unnecessary purchases. If you eliminate that waste, could you save $100 per month?
2. **Implement practices that save money:** Reduce the amount of food, energy, and water you waste every day. Cut back on unnecessary material purchases. Are you spending $100 less per month now that you're wasting fewer resources?
3. **Redirect waste to investment**: That $100 per month in avoided waste becomes your cash flow to fund your sustainability investments.
4. **Prioritize by return on investment**: Investments with the highest return generate the most in additional cash flow.
5. **Reinvest savings**: As sustainability investments generate returns, use that additional cash flow to take more steps that enable you to achieve goals that were previously out of reach.

Making It Stick

What is the difference between temporary changes and lasting transformation? Sustainable systems.

Habit Stacking

Attach new sustainable practices to existing routines:

- Carefully read and review your utility bills when you pay them
- Plan weekly meals during Sunday morning coffee
- Take out the compost when you put on headphones to listen to your favorite podcast

Visual Reminders

Make sustainable choices the obvious choices:

- Keep reusable shopping bags by the door or in your car
- Place composting pails next to your kitchen sink and bathroom sinks
- Post energy-saving reminders on your thermostat

Gamification

Make sustainability fun with friendly competitions:

- Track monthly utility bills and celebrate reductions
- Compete with friends and neighbors for the highest efficiency
- Create family challenges with rewards for sustainable choices

Regular Reviews

Schedule sustainability check-ins:

- Recalculate your sustainability score when you take more steps
- Identify new opportunities
- Adjust goals based on your track record

Family and Household Engagement

Sustainable living works best as a team sport. But how do you get reluctant family members on board?

Start with Benefits, Not Burdens

Explain what family members gain:

- "Fresh herbs make our food taste amazing" (not "we should grow our own food")
- "Walking together gives us time to talk" (not "we need to drive less")
- "This will save money for vacation" (not "we're spending too much on electricity")

Age-Appropriate Engagement

Young children (5-10): Make it magical

- Nature scavenger hunts in the yard
- Composting "feed the worm friends"
- Energy detective games

Tweens/Teens (11-18): Make it meaningful

- Gardening and backyard habitat projects
- Social media sustainability challenges
- Environmental club leadership
- Green career exploration

Partners/Spouses: Make it collaborative

- Joint goal setting
- Shared research on improvements
- Divided responsibilities by interest
- Celebrate wins together

Dealing with Resistance

When family members resist changes:

Listen first: What is the specific concern? Inconvenience? Cost? Skepticism about impact?

Start small: Propose trials—"Let's try composting for one month and see how it goes."

Offer choices: "Would you rather we focus on reducing energy use or cutting food waste?"

Show results: Share utility bill savings, Suspra Score improvements, wildlife returning to the yard

Respect boundaries: Some family members may never embrace certain practices. Do what you can agree on.

Making It Social

Extend sustainability beyond your household:

- Share successes on social media
- Host green potlucks with close friends
- Organize neighborhood tool shares
- Create walking groups
- Start community gardens

Technology Tools

Leverage technology to make sustainability easier.

- Smart thermostats that learn your schedule
- Automatic light dimmers based on daylight
- Water leak detectors with automatic shut-off
- Solar batteries that optimize energy use

From Measurement to Meaning

Your Suspra Score keeps you honest about whether you're living within Earth's means. But what do your measurements really mean?

The meaning is in the feeling you get when you realize you haven't burned any fossil fuel for an entire year. It's in your child's excitement to hear more birds singing in your native plant garden. It's in the satisfaction of a meal made entirely from your garden and local farms. It's in the pride of knowing you've helped other families in your community take their first steps on their own journeys to a sustainable future that benefits everyone.

Your Personal Implementation Roadmap

Let's make this happen with a step-by-step roadmap for the next year:

This Week
- ☐ Complete a Quick Start assessment at www.suspra.com
- ☐ Choose three "this week" practices from any pathway chapter
- ☐ Set up one visual reminder for a sustainable practice
- ☐ Share this book with one person

This Month
- ☐ Implement your three chosen practices consistently
- ☐ Complete a Regular assessment to calculate an evidence-based sustainability score
- ☐ Create your sustainability plan for your household

Next Three Months
- ☐ Master your initial three practices
- ☐ Add three more "this month" level practices
- ☐ Research costs and rebates for one major upgrade
- ☐ Engage your whole family in choosing your next steps
- ☐ Join a local sustainability group or online community

Next Six Months
- ☐ Measure your score again to see if you're making forward progress
- ☐ Complete one significant upgrade project
- ☐ Establish household sustainability routines
- ☐ Share your success story with others
- ☐ Update your sustainability plan now that you have some experience

One Year

☐ Calculate a detailed Suspra Score

☐ Celebrate improvements with family

☐ Document lessons learned

☐ Update your sustainability plan and set more ambitious goals

☐ Connect with community initiatives

The Compound Effect

Every positive change you make, no matter how small, contributes to a larger transformation. Your practices influence family, inspire neighbors, and inform friends. Your purchases signal manufacturers. Your votes shape policy. Your example proves what's possible.

To keep humanity within planetary boundaries so we can continue to live well on Earth, we don't need an occasional heroic individual making extreme sacrifices. We need millions of households like yours, making wise choices, measuring progress, and creating the conditions that make a sustainable future possible for everyone.

Your Earth Share Wisely Used

Before reading this book, you may not have realized that you—the same as everyone else on our planet—depend on a share of habitable land about the size of a soccer field. You now know a full range of practical strategies for living within the productive capacity of your Earth share so it can sustainably meet your needs. No guilt trips, no vague eco-tips, but twenty high-impact practices backed by science, a scoring system that measures real impact, and clarity about what actually matters.

Your Numbers Tell the Story

Your Suspra Score isn't a carbon footprint that measures only one dimension of your environmental impact. It's comprehensive data across seven pathways showing exactly where you stand relative to your equal share of our planet's ever-replenishing resources.

The idea that eating less beef has more total impact than all your recycling efforts combined isn't an opinion—it's measurement. The insight that your old refrigerator uses way more energy than a bigger new refrigerator is information you can act on. Knowledge is empowering. With wisdom you can move past eco-anxiety and confidently plan exactly what to do to make a positive difference.

A Truth About Sustainability

Sustainability is not really about making personal sacrifices for the common good, although that can be a strategy you pursue. Smart investments in better technology and techniques can be steps on your journey, too. LED bulbs provide better light while using 80% less energy. Heat pumps deliver more comfortable heating at a quarter of the energy cost. Induction cooking is faster, safer, and more precise. Walking and cycling make you healthier. Native plants require less maintenance while supporting hundreds more species than a lawn.

Resource conservation (doing without) costs nothing and requires nothing more than noble self-sacrifice, while resource efficiency (doing better) requires investment but maintains or increases your quality of life. Your circumstances determine your path. Both strategies lead to the same destination: an Earth that can sustain us all.

Your Impact Is Already Multiplying

Do you recall how individual water molecules can move just a little but still send powerful waves around the world? That's happening now as you choose to act. Every neighbor who sees butterflies in your native garden gets curious. Every friend who notices your solar array might ask questions. Every colleague who experiences your smooth, quiet electric ride might start imagining possibilities.

You're not preaching—you are demonstrating positive results. And just like those water molecules in a tsunami, your actions are influencing others to create a transformation none of you could achieve alone.

The World We're Creating

When billions of people make wise use of their Earth shares, we get the opposite of deprivation and disaster. We get cities where children can walk safely to school. We get delicious food grown in healthy soil. We get homes powered by sunshine and communities connected to nature. We get resilience, abundance, and a chance to reach our full potential as planetary caretakers.

Seven pathways to sustainability are your invitation to play a part in building the world you want your grandchildren and great-grandchildren to inherit. Every practice in this book already works successfully in someone's home. How well can they work in yours?

Appendix A: Your Earth Share

Imagine all of Earth's habitable land divided equally per person. Your portion—your *"Earth share"*—would be roughly the size of a soccer field (the exact size depending on where you draw the line between "habitable" and "uninhabitable" land). This isn't a policy proposal; it's a thought experiment to help you understand what constitutes living within a sustainable share of our planet's resources.

Of course, resources aren't equally distributed. Some parcels of land are more productive, and some are less productive than average. Some people consume more than average, while others subsist on less. But the fact is, if you're using more than average, someone else must make do with less. Our planet has a fixed size.

Sustainable Practice grounds our Suspra Score on the idea of many humans sharing one planet. A related approach, called the Ecological Footprint, estimates the global average productivity of a hectare of Earth's surface to determine the balance between the total supply and demand for nature. Every year, the Global Footprint Network announces Earth Overshoot Day to highlight how much faster humans are consuming ecological resources than Earth can provide them.

Planetary Math

Earth's total surface area is 51 billion hectares. Approximately 13 or 14 billion hectares of that is land, about one-third desert, another quarter mountainous, and some permanently frozen, leaving 6.4 billion hectares of *habitable* land for 8.2 billion people.

$$\frac{6.4 \: billion \: hectares}{8.2 \: billion \: people} = 0.78 \: hectares \: per \: person$$

Three-quarters of a hectare is a little bit more than one soccer field. As Earth's population grows to 10 billion, your Earth share will shrink to be smaller than a standard soccer field. Some sources cite higher figures of habitable land (assuming mountains and deserts are habitable) but even with this more generous definition, there's less than two soccer fields of habitable land available per person. In our main text, we round down to one to err on the side of safety and sustainability.

Note: I use scientific units throughout this appendix for clarity. A hectare is 100 meters by 100 meters, while a soccer field is about 100 meters by 70 meters.

What Your Earth Share Must Provide

Your Earth share is your life support system. Whatever you'd like to eat, drink, and do, a portion of our planet must provide it. The key insight for sustainability is that energy and materials flow naturally through every hectare of Earth. You can choose wise practices to live in harmony with these natural flows.

Habitable land can grow food, provide housing and recreation, generate energy, yield material resources, absorb and process waste, and provide habitat for diverse species. Ocean and inhospitable land could satisfy some of your needs; for example, you could obtain seafood and desalinated water from oceans, solar power from deserts, minerals from mountain peaks, and landfill capacity from wastelands. And one day, you could benefit from satellites in orbit around Earth generating solar power and housing data centers for artificial intelligence. Today, though, you meet most of your needs from habitable land on Earth.

Food Production

Growing crops and raising livestock requires habitable land. How much depends on your diet. Per person, a plant-based diet requires one-third of a soccer field. A beef-heavy diet requires two soccer fields, because it takes ten pounds of the kinds of plants that cattle can digest to produce one pound of edible beef. There simply isn't enough Earth for everyone to eat lots of beef at every meal; some of us must eat less beef than the average American, or we'd run out of habitable land for anything other than growing grass to feed and raise cattle.

Water Supply

Rain and snow fall on land and recharge groundwater supplies, with some of that water flowing in rivers to the sea. The global average precipitation rate is about one meter per year. Scaling that to the size of your home and yard, your sustainable water budget is 1,000 cubic meters per year. If you're using more water than this for your personal needs, you're taking water away from someone else. You're being extremely sustainable if you capture rainwater and snowmelt on your property, use it for all your needs, and then let your wastewater filter into your soil to replenish your local underground aquifers.

One-fifth of our world's population lives in water-scarce regions. In many places, we're "mining" ancient groundwater. What took millennia to accumulate, we're pumping out in decades. On Tuesday, you might be drinking water that fell as rain in 1776, and on Wednesday, you might be drinking the 1777 vintage. Fossil water—like the Ogallala Aquifer under America's Great Plains—is being depleted much faster than it naturally replenishes. If we don't get water-wise, we'll suck up our underground lakes, and our wells will start to go dry.

Energy and Power

Light energy constantly streams from our sun to our planet. You can turn this sunlight into electricity, store it in batteries, and use it to generate heat, spin motors, communicate, and compute.

Fossil fuel dominates the energy debate, but a "globally average" house (not in the sunniest location, but not in the shadiest) with rooftop solar modules and a whole-house battery can generate about one kilowatt of on-demand power per person (that is, electricity stored in batteries and available for use whenever desired), enough to satisfy household needs. Here are a few facts to help you understand the solar energy potential of your Earth share:

- A square meter of Earth (the size of a beach towel) receives one kilowatt of total solar power at noon on average.
- As of 2025, solar modules are about 20% efficient at converting sunlight to electricity (some are even more efficient than this).
- The capacity factor of a solar module depends on its location on Earth and orientation toward the sun. The global average solar capacity factor is about 16%.

Seven Pathways to Sustainable Living

To find the globally average solar power potential per square meter, multiply the amount of sunlight reaching the Earth's surface by solar module efficiency and capacity factor.

$$\frac{1\ kW}{m^2} \times 20\% \times 16\% = \frac{0.032\ kW}{m^2}$$

Sometimes we want to use power at night or when it's cloudy. For that, we need to store electricity in batteries. When we do that, we lose energy as heat in wires and battery cells. The round-trip efficiency of storing solar electricity in a battery is about 85%, i.e. if you use 100 kWh to charge a battery, when you discharge it you can expect to get about 85 kWh of useful electricity back and lose about 15 kWh as waste heat.

$$\frac{0.032\ kW}{m^2} \times 85\% = \frac{0.0272\ kW}{m^2}$$

A four-person home covers about 160 square meters, providing 40 square meters of roof space per person, yielding a battery-stored solar power budget of about 1 kilowatt.

$$\frac{0.0272\ kW}{m^2} \times 40\ m^2 = 1.088\ kW$$

If you keep your household power demand to one kilowatt per person, you're creating a world that can powered by endless clean solar energy stored in batteries, available on demand.

Biofuels—The Land Glutton

Now let's compare solar power to biofuels to understand how much wiser it is to control current than burn fuel. Per square meter of Earth used for energy, a battery-electric car that charges from solar power can go 350 times further than a car that burns corn ethanol.

Driving on Sunshine

- One square meter of land can provide 0.0272 kilowatts of on-demand battery-stored solar power.
- There are 8,760 hours per year.
- A new electric car can go about 5 kilometers per kWh of charge.

Your Earth Share

$$\frac{0.0272\ kW}{m^2} \times \frac{8{,}760\ hours}{year} \times \frac{5\ km}{kWh} = \frac{1{,}190\ km}{m^2\ year}$$

Driving on Corn

- One square meter of land can grow one kilogram of corn per year, from which 0.4 liters of ethanol can be produced.
- A new fuel-burning car can go about 8.5 kilometers per liter of ethanol.

$$\frac{1\ kg\ corn}{m^2\ year} \times \frac{0.4\ liters\ of\ ethanol}{kg\ of\ corn} \times \frac{8.5\ km}{liter\ of\ ethanol} = \frac{3.4\ km}{m^2\ year}$$

The comparison: Solar power enables 1,190 kilometers of driving per square meter while corn ethanol enables only 3.4—making solar 350 times more land-efficient for energy.

Why such a huge difference? Modern solar modules convert 20% of sunlight to electricity. Plants, by contrast, capture less than 1% of solar energy and convert it to biomass through photosynthesis. Then you lose more energy processing corn into ethanol, shipping the fuel, and burning it in an inefficient internal combustion engine that wastes most of the energy as heat.

Material Resources

Think of Earth's materials like a massive set of tiny Lego blocks. With the blocks (atoms) on our planet, mostly what we're doing is rearranging them into different structures. When you "consume" goods, you're not destroying atoms—you're just temporarily borrowing them in the form of a product, then sending them somewhere else when you're done with them. The fossil fuel industry, for instance, finds hydrogen and carbon atoms nicely arranged underground as oil and coal, then invites you to burn them, releasing the hydrogen atoms combined with oxygen as water and spreading the carbon atoms combined with oxygen throughout our atmosphere as carbon dioxide. But the atoms themselves? They're still here, just rearranged.

Only one industrial process actually destroys atoms on Earth. The nuclear industry takes big atoms and splits them into smaller atoms in a fission process to release energy. When uranium undergoes fission, it splits into smaller atoms plus neutrons and energy. Those uranium atoms are gone forever. Some nuclear proponents want to build reactors that bombard thorium with neutrons to create uranium, which then undergoes fission. This would permanently destroy Earth's limited supply of thorium.

Other nuclear proponents dream of fusion, which would combine isotopes of hydrogen (the smallest element) into helium (a larger element), releasing energy with fewer radioactive byproducts. This would draw down Earth's vast supply of hydrogen atoms and start creating new helium atoms. Fortunately, a natural fusion reaction is already safely happening exactly one astronomical unit away from Earth, so we can just tap into the endless energy that reactor (our sun) is reliably delivering to us daily.

Your Earth share provides all your material goods, but here's a crucial insight: some arrangements of atoms easily cycle through natural and industrial uses without causing negative side effects, while others create hazards. Water flows endlessly and naturally through cycles that sustain our ecosystem. But chlorofluorocarbons—once common in refrigerators and spray cans—float up to the stratosphere where ultraviolet light breaks off chlorine atoms that destroy our planet's ozone shield. You can help protect our planetary life-support systems by minimizing the hazardous materials in the mix you buy.

Consider PFAS—per- and polyfluoroalkyl substances—called "forever chemicals" because the carbon-fluorine bonds are among the strongest in chemistry. These molecules don't break down naturally very often. Instead, they accumulate in water, in animals, and in humans. To recover the atoms in PFAS requires extreme measures to break the carbon-fluorine bonds: incineration at over 1,000°C or plasma treatment that rips apart molecules with ionized gas. Every non-stick pan, water-resistant jacket, and grease-proof food wrapper containing PFAS adds to a pollution problem if those chemicals aren't carefully collected and processed. Carbon and fluorine atoms aren't always hazardous, but they are when we combine them into PFAS.

Your Sustainable Materials Budget

Ecological regeneration is a natural process that harnesses solar energy to organize atoms into useful arrangements—photosynthesis building cellulose in plants, bacteria fixing nitrogen in soil, oysters filtering water while building shells from calcium carbonate. Your Earth share consists of many kinds of atoms and many solar-powered natural "assembly lines" that can produce many different types of materials, including wood and natural fibers.

Let's explore some examples. The average American currently consumes about 100 kilograms of materials per day. That alone is a problem: it would be more sustainable to consume at a lower rate. But how much material is not the end of the story. What kind of material matters, too.

A Tale of Two T-Shirts

An organic cotton t-shirt is grown from soil and air using solar power, and becomes soil and air when composted. Its atoms cycle naturally. A polyester t-shirt is made from petroleum, sheds microplastics with every wash, never fully decomposes, and releases toxic fumes if burned. Its atoms become pollution. Both shirts clothe you, but one borrows atoms temporarily and returns them to nature, while the other locks them into problematic arrangements for centuries.

The Aluminum Can Miracle

Metals are where material management becomes almost magical. Making aluminum from bauxite ore requires a significant amount of energy—about 15 kWh per kilogram. But once made, aluminum can be recycled indefinitely using just 0.75 kWh of energy per kilogram. The atoms never degrade and are relatively easily recovered and rearranged. A single aluminum can, recycled every two months, could provide beverage containers for billions of years using just 0.001 kW of battery-stored solar power. Recycled aluminum atoms can provide frames for solar modules for even less power, because we only need new frames every thirty years rather than every two months. Compare that to a plastic bottle: even if recycled once, it degrades into lower-quality plastic, then becomes a problem that requires careful and energy-intensive processing to return to productive use.

Waste Absorption

When you throw something "away," you're just moving atoms from one place to another on Earth. Atoms don't leave our planet (except for those we convert to energy in nuclear reactors, or the few spacecraft we send beyond Earth's gravity well). Every atom in your garbage can, recycling bin, or compost pile stays right here on our planet, available for use by future generations.

Banana peels aren't "waste"—they are soil nutrients taking a trip through your kitchen. Aluminum cans aren't waste—they are about half an Avogadro's number of aluminum atoms that can be fashioned into new cans or other items for billions of years. Even sewage isn't waste—it's mostly organic matter that can fertilize fields or forests.

Nature's Recycling Rates

Per square meter of Earth, you can fully compost about 500 kilograms of organic matter annually—including food waste, feces, paper, and yard trimmings. When you compost, you're helping nature do what it does naturally, but much faster and in a controlled location. Modern composting toilets and backyard composters turn "waste" into a valuable soil amendment. Methane digesters take a detour, halting decomposition with four hydrogen atoms still connected to one carbon atom (a methane molecule), before returning the remaining nutrients to soil.

Carbon Dioxide: You eat glucose and other carbon-containing molecules for energy, breathing in oxygen to enable your metabolism and breathing out about a kilogram of carbon dioxide per day. (You might think food goes in, poop comes out, but poop is the part of what you eat that your body can't use for energy. Over the course of a week, your exhaled breath normally weighs more than your poop.) Plants absorb carbon dioxide and water, and use solar power to produce the food you eat. That is a sustainable carbon cycle: food goes in your body, carbon dioxide comes out, carbon dioxide goes into plants, food comes out. But if you burn fossil fuels, you release ancient carbon that's been sequestered (locked away) for millions of years underground, adding more carbon to our atmosphere than plants can absorb.

Your Earth share can sequester about half a kilogram of carbon dioxide per square meter per year, thanks to plants and other organisms that store carbon in their tissues and in soil. If you burn too much fossil fuel too quickly, you overwhelm nature's carbon dioxide absorption capacity. It's like opening boxes of Lego blocks and dumping them out all at once. If you dumped out just one box every day, your shop vac could keep up. But if you dump out many boxes every day, you overwhelm your vacuum's capacity, and the blocks will start to pile up.

Water Processing: Soil is nature's water filter. One hundred square meters of wetland can process all the wastewater from a family of four, delivering nutrients to plants (rather than running off to waterways), breaking down pathogens, and returning clean water to the cycle.

Troublesome Substances

Some arrangements of atoms are particularly troublesome:

Radioactive Waste: When we split atoms for energy, the smaller atoms remain dangerously radioactive for millennia. Your Earth share has no natural way to process this—to protect human health, radioactive elements must be isolated from the biosphere until they have decayed to elements that don't radiate so much damaging energy.

Persistent Synthetic Chemicals: Some molecular arrangements we create—like PFAS "forever chemicals"—form bonds so strong that nature has few tools to break them, so they accumulate. Once these synthetic molecules become dispersed and embedded in our ecosystem, it becomes an impossible task to collect them all so that we can safely break them down.

Mixed Materials: Plastic packaging contains many different elements bonded in complex ways. Separating them for recycling requires much more energy than extracting new materials.

Habitat

Just as your body needs beneficial bacteria to digest food and fight disease, Earth needs diverse organisms to cycle nutrients, purify water, pollinate plants, and maintain soil health. You can't build on, pave over, or mow your entire Earth share without undermining your own well-being. Some portion of the soccer field sustaining you must also sustain the organisms that create the necessary conditions for your survival.

Free Services That Nature Provides

Every square meter of natural habitat works around the clock. Wetlands—even a small rain garden—filter water naturally and keep nutrients from running off. Trees and plants remove carbon dioxide and release oxygen while filtering out pollutants. Bacteria, fungi, insects, and worms break down organic matter, cycle nutrients, and maintain soil structure that prevents erosion and stores water. Pollinators visit flowers to feed while inadvertently enabling plants to set fruit and reproduce.

Why Biodiversity Matters

Monocultures—single species dominating an area—are fragile. When disease strikes or conditions change, the entire system can collapse. But diverse ecosystems are resilient. Wild habitats maintain a genetic library of traits that might prove essential as conditions change. If one species struggles, others fill its role. This redundancy isn't inefficient—it's insurance against catastrophe. Consider what happened during Ireland's potato famine: when *Phytophthora infestans* blight arrived, it destroyed most of the harvest because most Irish farms had planted only a single type of potato that was susceptible.

Indicator Species Tell the Story

Certain species reveal ecosystem health. Frogs and salamanders, breathing through their skin, are among the first creatures to die when water becomes polluted. Lichens on trees indicate clean air—they can't survive where air pollution is high. Birds are undeniable indicators. A yard with diverse bird species has adequate food sources, nesting sites, and clean water. A dawn chorus of birdsong is evidence that your local ecosystem is functioning well.

Your Earth Share

How Much Space Does Nature Need?

Below a threshold of habitat, animals can't find mates or establish new territories, and populations become isolated and vulnerable. To be sure you're providing enough for healthy biodiversity, allow half of your Earth share to harbor native species. This doesn't mean you can't use this land at all. An organic orchard with native fruit and nut trees provides habitat and food. A meadow of native plants that you enjoy for the view supports far more biodiversity than a lawn. Even a windowsill flower box or a nesting area under a porch provides living space for other species.

Connectivity is key. Your wild spaces become far more valuable when they connect to your neighbors' wild spaces, creating corridors through which species can move. Your land isn't an island—it's part of a continent-wide network of habitats.

The Power of Your Choices

You can meet all your needs using your own soccer-field-sized share of Earth or force someone else to sacrifice some of theirs. Living brilliantly within your environmental means isn't about deprivation—it's about choosing wise practices. Knowing that you can drive 350 times farther on solar electricity than biofuels from the same land, that an aluminum can is easily recycled while a plastic bottle becomes problematic pollution, and that even small patches of habitat can mean life or death for millions of native species, makes your path forward clearer.

Your Earth share isn't an impossible limit; it's enough for a magnificent, rewarding life well lived. The atoms are all here, the sun's energy arrives fresh every morning, nature's recycling systems work tirelessly—and this book is available to guide you to align your practices with natural flows. It's your choice: how will you use your Earth share?

Appendix B: Planetary Boundaries

Planetary boundaries are operating limits, based on scientific evidence, for human pressure on nine Earth systems that keep our planet safe and stable for human civilization.

1. **Climate change**
   Adding greenhouse gases to Earth's atmosphere traps heat that would otherwise escape into space.
2. **Biosphere integrity disruption**
   Driving species to extinction threatens the energy balance and chemical cycles of Earth.
3. **Novel entities**
   Introducing novel synthetic chemicals into our environment, mobilizing materials in novel ways, and modifying genomes differently than natural evolution all change the functioning of the Earth system.
4. **Stratospheric ozone depletion**
   Thinning of the ozone layer, high in the atmosphere, primarily due to synthetic chemicals, allows more harmful ultraviolet radiation to reach Earth's surface.
5. **Atmospheric aerosol loading**
   Changes in airborne particles from human activities alter temperature and precipitation patterns.
6. **Ocean acidification**
   Increasing carbon dioxide concentrations in the atmosphere increases the acidity of surface waters.
7. **Biogeochemical flow changes**
   Dumping phosphorus into the ocean and converting stable nitrogen from the atmosphere into bioreactive forms both disrupt nutrient balances for living organisms.
8. **Freshwater change**
   Draining wetlands, altering river flows, and extracting water from aquifers affect carbon sequestration, reduce biodiversity, and shift precipitation levels.
9. **Land-system change**
   Clearing natural ecosystems for agriculture, roads, and buildings destroys habitat, reduces biodiversity, affects carbon sequestration, and disrupts natural water cycles.

Your Earth Share

In 2009, Johan Rockström and colleagues first described the planetary boundaries framework in a *Nature* paper. It was updated in 2015 by Will Steffen and team, who emphasized that climate change and biosphere integrity are the "core" boundaries that strongly shape the rest. The most recent global update in 2023 found that stratospheric ozone is recovering, ocean acidification is close to the edge, and aerosols are at safe levels in some regions; for the remaining six boundaries, Earth is in the danger zone.

How boundaries connect to your practices

1. **Climate change:** All practices help.
2. **Biosphere integrity disruption:** Eat more plants, support regenerative farming, and landscape with native plants. (*Practices: #4, #5, #11*)
3. **Novel entities:** Buy less, avoid single-use plastics, choose safer products. (*Practices: #1, #6, #7*)
4. **Stratospheric ozone depletion:** Clean with safe products, handle refrigerants safely. (*Practices: #7, #13, #15, #18*)
5. **Atmospheric aerosols:** Compost, walk, cycle, or take public transit for local errands, electrify, and go solar. (*Practices: #2, #3, #13, #14, #16, #17, #18, #19*)
6. **Ocean acidification:** All practices help.
7. **Biogeochemical flow changes:** Compost, eat more plants, garden wisely, and support regenerative farming, drink more tap water, clean with safe products, and landscape using organic methods. (*Practices: #2, #4, #5, #6, #7, #11*)
8. **Freshwater change:** Plant drought-resilient landscapes, wash clothes in an efficient machine, go solar, and flush water-efficient toilets. (*Practices: #11, #12, #19, #20*)
9. **Land-system change:** Eat more plants, grow a garden, drink more tap water, recycle metal, cardboard, and glass. (*Practices: #4, #5, #6, #8*)

Planetary boundaries are the science of sustainability. The practices in this book are the step-by-step ways to steer your household, workplace, and community toward a more sustainable future for everyone.

Appendix C: Seven Pathways

Our Seven Pathways framework transforms the hitherto overwhelming challenge of sustainability into a practical journey you can successfully undertake. Visit www.suspra.com to measure where you are now and chart your course to live within planetary boundaries.

Community Pathway

Goal: A community that understands and practices environmental sustainability

When you coordinate sustainable practices among your community, your actions resonate into transformative change—like water molecules nudging their neighbors to create waves that circle the globe.

Sustainability Knowledge Score

Milestone	Score (% on tests)
Have Basic Awareness	20%
Understand Core Concepts	50%
Comprehend Systems Thinking	75%
Can Teach Others	100%

High-Impact Practices Score

Milestone	Score (% of 20 practices)
Starting Out	25%
Building Good Habits	50%
Reaching Sustainability	75%
Fully Practicing the Basics	100%

Social Interaction

Milestone	Score (volunteer hours)
Building the Volunteer Habit	50
Estimated U.S. Average	66
Active Volunteer	100
Volunteer Leader	200

Food Pathway

Goal: Eating within Earth's sustainable agricultural capacity

If everyone ate like Americans, we'd need to colonize other planets to raise enough beef cattle. Plant-based diets can feed everyone using existing farmland while restoring ecosystems.

Food Waste Rate

Milestone	Score (% of food eaten)
Estimated U.S. Average	62%
Reducing Waste	70%
Mindful Consumption	80%
Minimal Waste	90%
Masterful Management	98%

Eco-Friendly Ingredients

Milestone	Score (% of weekly meals)
Raising Awareness	60%
Conscious Eater	75%
Very Diligent	90%
Fully Responsible	100%

Plant-Based Meals

Milestone	Score (% of weekly meals)
Estimated U.S. Average	16.5%
Flexitarian	50%
Plant-forward	70%
Nearly Vegetarian	85%
Fully Vegetarian	100%

Regeneratively Grown Food

Milestone	Score (% of food budget)
Estimated U.S. Average	6%
Some Organic	25%
Half Organic	50%
Mostly Organic	75%
Fully Organic	100%

Water Pathway

Goal: Respecting and protecting natural freshwater limits

If your household consumes no more than 100 liters of water daily per person, you're helping to protect aquifers that took millennia to fill.

Daily Water Use

Milestone	Score (daily liters)
Estimated U.S. Average	310
Becoming Conscious	190
Becoming Efficient	130
Becoming Sustainable	100
Water Wise	75

Biodegradable Cleaning and Hygiene Products

Milestone	Score (% of products used)
Taking Some Steps	25%
Halfway There	50%
Mostly Natural	75%
Fully Biodegradable	100%

Movement Pathway

Goal: Planet-friendly mobility that strengthens community

Moving 40 kilometers per day on average or less, mostly under human power and driving fully electric, respects planetary boundaries.

Average Daily Distance Traveled

Milestone	Score (kilometers per day)
Estimated U.S. Average	65
Reducing Travel	55
Local Focused	40
Community Grounded	30
Walkable Life	16

Active Transportation (Walking or Cycling)

Milestone	Score (% of trips)
Estimated U.S. Average	11%
Sometimes Active	25%
Often Active	50%
Active First	80%
Car Free	100%

Electric Vehicle Miles

Milestone	Score (% of distance driven)
Estimated U.S. Average	<2%
Happy Hybrid	30%
Plug Preference	60%
Battery Bravura	100%

Your Earth Share

Energy Pathway

Goal: Thriving within Earth's solar power energy budget

Your sustainable power budget is one kilowatt—achievable through efficiency and 100% solar electricity stored in batteries.

Power Demand

Milestone	Score (kW average)
Estimated U.S. Average	3.75
Reducing Waste	2.50
Becoming Efficient	1.75
Sustainable	1.00
Energy Wise	0.50

Home Electrification

Milestone	Score (% of energy)
Estimated U.S. Average	40%
Getting Started	50%
Making Progress	60%
Mostly Electric	80%
Fully Electrified	100%

Seven Pathways to Sustainable Living

Solar Power

Milestone	Score (% of energy)
Estimated U.S. Average	5%
Adding Solar	15%
Green Power	50%
Mostly Solar	75%
Fully Solar	100%

Goods Pathway

Goal: Material flows that safely cycle

Your sustainable consumption budget is 25 daily kilograms that cycle safely through natural composting and industrial recycling systems.

Material Consumption

Milestone	Score (daily kg per person)
Estimated U.S. Average	48
Reducing Consumption	40
Moderate Consumer	30
Sustainable Consumer	25
Minimalist	15

Composting (Natural Process) Rate

Milestone	Score (% waste composted)
Estimated U.S. Average	8.5%

Milestone	Score (% waste composted)
Better Than Average	10%
Making Progress	15%
Good Practices	25%
Excellent Practices	40%
Super Practices	60%

Recycling (Industrial Process) Rate

Milestone	Score (% waste recycled)
Estimated U.S. Average	32%
Better Than Average	35%
Sustainable Recycling Rate	40%
Overshoot (Compost More)	50%

Reuse Rate

Milestone	Score (% reused)
Estimated U.S. Average	10%
Starting to Reuse	20%
Building Good Habits	30%
Regular Reuser	50%
Reuse Economizer	75%
Ultimate Reuse Expert	100%

Sustainable Materials

Milestone	Score (% safe and manageable)
Good	50%
Better	75%
Excellent	90%
Perfect	100%

Habitat Pathway

Goal: Shelter that enhances rather than destroys ecosystems

Your sustainable habitat budget is 50 square meters for your housing, managing your land wisely to support native biodiversity.

Your Earth Share

Living Space

Milestone	Score (square meters)
Estimated U.S. Average	85
Somewhat Space Efficient	75
Downsizing	65
Sustainable Housing Size	50
Tiny Home	37

Green Building Certification

Milestone	Score (standards value)
Level 1 Standard	1
Level 2 Standard	2
Level 3 Standard	3
Level 4 Standard	4

Native Habitat

Milestone	Score (% of property)
Estimated U.S. Average	5%
Some Native Areas	25%
Half Wild	50%
Mostly Natural	75%
Wildlife Refuge	90%

Land Management

Milestone	Score (% organic practices)
Estimated U.S. Average	10%
Reducing Chemicals	50%
Mostly Organic	75%
Fully Organic	100%

Appendix D: Suggested Resources

The facts and figures in this book are drawn from the ongoing research we conduct at Sustainable Practice. If you'd like to do your own research or learn more about any of the statistics or ideas you've come across in this book, here are some resources we recommend.

Artificial Intelligence

Large language models provide access to distilled versions of the world's knowledge. By visiting a website or using a "chatbot" app, you can have a conversation and ask for research reports on any topic. Before relying on anything a chatbot tells you, verify the information from another source.

- ChatGPT (chatgpt.com)
- Claude (claude.ai)
- Gemini (gemini.google.com)

Data

Curated data sets provide access to facts and figures derived from the efforts of public and private research.

- Our World in Data (ourworldindata.org)
- U.S. Energy Information Administration (eia.gov)
- World Environmental Situation Room (wesr.unep.org)

Environmental Frameworks and Projects

Our Earth share and pathways concepts draw from established environmental frameworks and projects, such as these.

- Ecological Footprint (footprintnetwork.org)
- Planetary Boundaries (stockholmresilience.org)
- Project Drawdown (drawdown.org)
- Rewiring America (rewiringamerica.org)

INDEX

A
Active transportation, 4, 30-36
  bicycling, 4, 31-36
  walking, 31-36
Air sealing, 4, 39, 43-46
Aluminum recycling, 49

B
Battery storage, 44
Biodegradable products, 4, 47, 53
Biodiversity, 55

C
California plastic bag ban, 8
Calculations, 78-82
Carbon footprint, 5, 39-46
Circular economy, 47
Clean energy. See Solar power
Climate change, 2, 3
Cold water washing, 39, 43
Community, 4, 7-14
  building networks, 10
  creating waves, 14
  environmental volunteer projects, 13
  growing sustainable communities, 11
  knowledge sharing, 12
Composting, 4, 48-49

D
Dashboard indicators
  community, 11-12
  food, 18-19
  water, 26
  movement, 32-33
  energy, 42-43
  goods, 50-51

habitat, 57-58

E
Earth share concept, 2, 9, 15, 36, 38, 45, 47, 48, 55, 63, 76-79, 84, 88
Earth share calculations, 78-88
Eco-friendly cleaning products, 24, 27
Eco-friendly food ingredients, 16
Electric vehicles, 4, 31, 32, 34, 35
Electrification, 38, 40, 41, 44, 45
   cooking appliances, 41, 44, 45
   heat pumps, 38, 40, 41, 44, 45
   water heaters, 40
   energy efficiency, 37, 38, 39-41, 39
   ENERGY STAR appliances, 27
   LED lighting, 38, 39
Energy pathway strategies, 38

F
Filters, water, 17, 20
Financial Planning, 68-70
Food pathway strategies and practices, 16, 19
   plant-based meals, 4, 15, 16, 19, 20, 21, 22
   drinking water, 4, 17, 18, 20
   growing/buying local organic, 4, 16, 17, 20

G
Goods pathway strategies, 48
   eco-friendly goods, 48
Green building, 56
Green building certifications, 58
Greywater systems, 28, 29

H
Heat pumps, 40, 41, 44, 45
High-impact practices (20 total), 4

I
Induction cooking, 41

Insulation, 4, 39, 43-46
Invasive species, 60

L
Landscaping, 56
LED lighting, 4, 38, 39, 43, 45
Leaks, water, 26, 27

M
Movement pathway strategies, 31
   electric driving, 31
   exercise while moving, 31
   reducing car travel miles, 33, 34

N
Native plants, 56, 61

O
Organic food, 16, 17, 20, 21

P
PFAS, 83
Planetary boundaries, 2, 3, 9, 89, 90
Plant-based diet benefits, 4, 15, 16, 22
Plastic recycling problems, 49
Public transit, 4, 31, 34, 35

Q
QR codes for online tools
  Community, 13, 14
  Food, 18, 19
  Water, 26
  Movement, 32, 33
  Energy, 42, 43
  Goods, 50, 51
  Habitat, 57, 58

R
Recycling, 4, 48, 49, 50, 51, 52
Regenerative farming, 16, 17
Renewable energy. See Solar power
Renovating wisely, 56

S
Safe cleaning products 4, 48,
Sealing and insulation 4, 39
Seven pathways framework, 4
   Community, 7-14
   Food, 13-22
   Water, 23-29
   Movement, 30-36
   Energy, 37-46
   Goods, 47-54
   Habitat, 55-62
Solar power 4, 37, 38, 41, 42, 44, 45, 46
   community solar, 42
   cost reduction, 41, 44, 45
   rooftop systems, 44
SusPra score, 63-67
Sustainable shelter, 56
Sustainability indicators. See Dashboard   Indicators
Sustainability journal, 11
Sustainability score calculator, 11

T
Toilets, water-efficient, 25
Transportation. See Movement pathway
Twenty high-impact practices, 4

W
Walking and cycling, 31
Waste management, 48-50
Water conservation, 23-29
   community water conservation, 28
   efficient fixtures, 27

leak detection, 26
rainwater collection, 28
Water heaters,40
Water pathway strategies, 24
  efficiency optimization, 25, 26, 27
Water-efficient toilets , 25

Appendices
Appendix A (Earth share calculations), 78-88
Appendix B (planetary boundaries), 89, 90
Appendix C (Seven Pathways scoring), 91-101
Appendix D (resources), 102

Notes and Observations

Use these pages to keep a sustainability journal for yourself or to share your thoughts for the next person to read this book!

Notes and Observations

Notes and Observations

About the Author

For over thirty years, Fred Horch has dedicated his professional and personal life to empowering people to not only envision a sustainable future but to take effective action to help create it. A sustainability advisor and small business owner, Fred is the former proprietor of F.W. Horch Sustainable Goods & Supplies, a retail store specializing in sustainable living, and is currently one of the owners of Spark Applied Efficiency, an electrical contracting firm with a mission to help people create more valuable and sustainable businesses through efficiency.

In 2023, with Peggy Siegle, Fred founded Sustainable Practice to provide education through publications and presentations for individuals and organizations committed to environmental sustainability. Before he began working in the sustainability field, he was a corporate attorney, Internet project manager, and computer network sysadmin.

Fred earned a Juris Doctor degree from the University of California, Berkeley, School of Law, and a Bachelor of Arts degree in Political Science, with concentrations in international relations and computer science, from Swarthmore College. He has studied and lived in France, the Soviet Union, Japan, Chile, and New Zealand. In the United States, he has lived in Utah, Pennsylvania, California, North Carolina, New York, and Maine.

When Fred is not working on business projects, writing about sustainability, or developing software with the help of leading-edge AI, he is busy as a father of three children, a Rotarian, and a Master Gardener volunteer, living with his good-natured wife Hadley in a solar-powered all-electric house built in 1828 in Brunswick, Maine.

More from Sustainable Practice

Sustainable Practices: Your Handbook for Effective Action

Join a community of positive change agents who are creating a better future for everyone on Earth. Transform your community into a catalyst for global environmental stewardship. Get our most comprehensive "how-to" handbook for the serious sustainability practitioner.

2025 edition, 582 pages

Bite-sized Changes, Big Impact: Your Sustainable Food Journey

Every meal you prepare is a powerful choice. Your fork can either support agricultural practices that restore our planet or contribute to its destruction. What if every bite you take could help create a more sustainable world?

2025 edition, 24 pages

Creating Wonderful Waste: Your Guide to Sustainable Composting

Every banana peel you throw away could end up in a landfill, generating methane—a greenhouse gas 25 times more potent than carbon dioxide. What if you could transform those peels into rich, life-giving soil that captures carbon instead?

2025 edition, 24 pages

Money That Matters: Your Guide to Sustainable Finances

Every dollar you spend or save is a powerful choice. Your money can either fund practices that protect our planet or finance its destruction. What if every financial decision you made could help build a more sustainable world?

2025 edition, 24 pages

"One Step This Week"

Get a practical action idea for sustainability delivered to your e-mail inbox every Sunday morning. Available on Substack and Medium.

For more information, please visit us at

www.SustainablePractice.Life

www.ingramcontent.com/pod-product-compliance
Lightning Source LLC
Chambersburg PA
CBHW070639030426
42337CB00020B/4076